ROSS WILLIS

Ross is a playwright from Bristol. His debut play *Wolfie* premiered at Theatre503 to great critical acclaim, setting him out as 'a fresh and fearless voice' in British theatre. The play won Best New Play at both the Writers' Guild Awards and the Off-West End Awards 2020 and also earned him a nomination for Best Writer at the 2019 Stage Debut Awards and Most Promising Playwright at the Evening Standard Theatre Awards.

He won the 2019 Royal Court and Kudos Fellowship and the 2019 Channel 4 Playwright Award. Ross took part in the writers' room for *The Outlaws* created by Stephen Merchant and is currently under commission to the Royal Court, the Orange Tree Theatre, Soho Theatre, Paines Plough, LAMDA and the Almeida Theatre.

Ross Willis

WONDER BOY

NICK HERN BOOKS
London
www.nickhernbooks.co.uk

A Nick Hern Book

Wonder Boy first published in Great Britain as a paperback original in 2022 by Nick Hern Books Limited, The Glasshouse, 49a Goldhawk Road, London W12 8QP

Wonder Boy copyright © 2022 Ross Willis

Ross Willis has asserted his right to be identified as the author of this work

Cover image: Ben Robins

Designed and typeset by Nick Hern Books, London
Printed in Great Britain by Mimeo Ltd, Huntingdon, Cambridgeshire PE29 6XX

A CIP catalogue record for this book is available from the British Library

ISBN 978 1 84842 954 3

Woodland
CARBON
www.woodlandcarbon.co.uk
NICK HERN BOOKS
Printed on Carbon Captured paper

Wonder Boy was first performed at Bristol Old Vic on 10 March 2022 (previews from 5 March), with the following cast:

SONNY	Raphel Famotibe
CAPTAIN CHATTER	Ramesh Meyyappan
ROSHI	Juliet Agnes
WAINWRIGHT	Amanda Lawrence
FISH/SONNY'S MUM	Jenny Fitzpatrick
MUSICIANS	Benji Bower
	Will Bower

All other parts played by members of the company

Writer	Ross Willis
Director	Sally Cookson
Set and Costume Designer	Katie Sykes
Composer	Benji Bower
Lighting Designer	Aideen Malone
Sound Designer	Jonathan Everett
Caption and Video Design	Tom Newell of Limbic Cinema
Associate Director	Max Sutherland
Movement Director	Laila Diallo
Deaf Consultant	David Ellington
Casting Director	Jessica Straker
Costume and Wigs Supervisor	Sophia Khan
Fight Director	Claire Llewellyn
Speech and Language Therapists	Debbie Mason and Anna Prince
Emerging Creative Artist Placement	Ciaran O'Breen

Acknowledgements

Thanks to Sally Cookson, Tom Morris, Sian Weeding and everyone at the Bristol Old Vic. Ned Bennett, Nic Connaughton, Alex Corey, Lisa Goldman, Jules Haworth, Yasmin Joseph, Dennis Kelly, Bec Martin, Ali McDowall, Claire O'Reilly, Tom Powell, Lisa Spirling, Julie Taymor, Sarah Liisa Wilkinson and everyone at Nick Hern Books, and the brilliant company of *Wonder Boy*.

R.W.

Characters

SONNY
CAPTAIN CHATTER
ROSHI
WAINWRIGHT
FISH
SONNY'S MUM
WILLIAM SHAKESPEARE
THE SKULL
THE LETTER A

Notes on Text

Sonny has a stammer which consists of repeating phrases and involuntary pauses.

The actor should of course find their own rhythm as what is written is purely a guide, Obvs.

Wainwright sometimes stammers on the letter H. It is a stammer with no tension.

Sliding onto a word is when you elongate the initial sound of the word.

Scenes should bleed into each other.

Moments of magic should feel makeshift and created by the company in the moment.

This text went to press before the end of rehearsals and so may differ slightly from the play as performed.

A Prologue

SONNY. Continuing the adventures of Captain Chatter with the amazing power of SPEECH!

CAPTAIN CHATTER *dramatically appears.*

The amazing power to ask the bus driver for a ticket.

CAPTAIN CHATTER. RETURN TO THE CENTRE PLEASE! *POW!!!!!*

Everyone loses their shit.

SONNY. The amazing power to make small talk.

CAPTAIN CHATTER. THE WEATHER! BAM!!!!!

THE NICE WEATHER! THE BAD WEATHER! WHAM!!!!!

THE FACT THAT THERE'S WEATHER! *KAZAM!!!!*

Everyone loses their shit even more.

SONNY. The amazing power to read in class.

CAPTAIN CHATTER. THE OWL AND THE PUSSY-CAT WENT TO SEA IN A BEAUTIFUL PEA-GREEN BOAT, THEY TOOK SOME HONEY, AND PLENTY OF MONEY, WRAPPED UP IN A FIVE-POUND NOTE. *SMASH!!!!!*

HOLY FUCK THIS GUY IS AMAZING!!!!!!!!!!!!!

SONNY. The amazing power to say tongue twisters.

CAPTAIN CHATTER. SHE SELLS SEASHELLS BY THE SEASHORE. KA-BOOM!!!!!!

1

Outside the Deputy Headteacher's office.
After school.

ROSHI *is waiting.* SONNY *enters.*
His shirt is covered with splatters of blood.

SONNY *I-I-I-I-I-I-I-I-I-I-I-I-I-I-I-I-I–* (*Trying to say the word 'Is'.*)

    UGH!!

    I-I-I-I-I-I-I-I-I-I-I-I-I-I-I-I-IS THH THH-THH-THH-THH- this the De– (*Trying to say the word 'Deputy'.*)

SONNY *starts stammering a long repetition of the letter D.*

ROSHI *doesn't hide her shock over* SONNY*'s stammer.*

    *F-F-F-F-F-F-F-*FORGET I-I-I-I-I-it!

SONNY *runs away.*

ROSHI. COME BACK!

    I'M GONNA HOLD MY BREATH UNTIL YOUS COME BACK AND THEN WHEN I DIE IT'S GONNA BE YOUR FAULT.

ROSHI *holds her breath.*

SONNY *slowly returns.*
Full of embarrassment, he looks to the floor.

SONNY. *I-I-I-I-I-I-I-I-I-I-I-Is-*this the De–

    *D-D-D-*DEPUTY *H-H-H* HEAD'S *O-O-O-O-O-O-O-O-*OFFICE?

ROSHI. OH.
    YEAH.
    I'M STARVIN.
    YOUS GOT ANY FOOD ON YOUS?

SONNY *shakes his head no.*

WANNA KNOW WHAT I'D LOVE?
TOMATO KETCHUP.
IT'S MY THING
IT DEFINES ME.
LIKE WHENEVER I'M AT A BARBECUE EVERYONE
ALWAYS GOES
'HERE GOES ROSHI WITH THE KETCHUP, IT'S HER
THING, IT DEFINES HER.'

SONNY *takes out a pad and pencil and begins to draw.*
ROSHI *tries to have a peek which makes* SONNY
uncomfortable.

I KNOW YOUS DON'T I?

SONNY *desperately shakes his head no. She doesn't know
him. Nobody can know him.*

YEAH I KNOW YOUS! YOUS LIVES ON MY ESTATE?
YOUS ALWAYS SIT OUTSIDE DRAWIN.

SONNY. !!!

ROSHI. OI YOUS LIVES ON MY ESTATE!?

SONNY *nods yes. He's been caught out. Fuck.*

AND YOUR MUM'S LIKE 'COME ON IN'.

SONNY. *S-S-S-S-S-S-S-S-S-S-S-*SHE'S *NHH-NHHHHH-*NOT
*MMM-*MY MUM!

ROSHI. WELL YOUR NOT-MUM THEN.
DIDN'T I SAY I KNOW YOUS? WHAT BLOCK YOUS IN?

SONNY. *T-t-t-t-*the one that *r-r-*reeks like –

D–	
D–	
D–	ROSHI. DINOSAUR!?
D–	DOG!?
D–	DECEASED!
D–	DRAGON!?

AGHHHHHHHHH!!!!!!!!!!!

(*An involuntary pause on the word 'piss'.*)

P-p-p-p-p-piss.

ROSHI. YOUS FUNNY!
THEY ALL REEK LIKE PISS!
PUDDLES OF PISS!
PISSTASTIC!
URINAL LOT OF TROUBLE IF YOUS LIVE IN OUR
ESTATE.

ROSHI *laughs at her own pun.*
Her laugh makes SONNY *laugh.*
SONNY *opens his mouth but has an involuntary pause.*
ROSHI *doesn't notice and speaks over him.*

IT'S GETTIN *EXCREMENTALLY WORSE!!!!!!!!!!*

SONNY. *I-I-I-I*-it's been – (*Trying to say his AMAZING pun
'Shattered to faeces'.*)
SHH-SHH-SHH-SHH-SHH-SHH-SHH–
UGH!

ROSHI *is losing interest.*

SONNY *stops. He silently begs his mouth to be able to
deliver this joke.*

Please let it work. Please let it work. Please let it work.

I-I-I-I-it's been *SHH-SHH-SHH-SHH-SHH-SHH-SHH-
SHH!!!*

ROSHI. HEY IS THAT BLOOD!?

SONNY. *Y-y-y*– (*He sighs and just nods instead.*)

ROSHI. COOL!
YOUS SHOULD LET ME PIERCE YOUR EAR. YOUS
LOOK WELL CUTE WITH A PIERCIN
I TRIED TO PRACTISE ON MY MUM BUT SHE WOKE
UP.

SONNY. *Whhhhh-whhh*-why yous *h-h*-here?

ROSHI. YOUS KNOW CHANTELLE GREEN FROM YEAR
10 RIGHT?
HER DOG WENT MISSING AND SHE PUT UP
POSTERS.
BUT I'M NOT SURE YOUS *REALLY* MISS YOUR DOG
IF YOUS USIN COMIC SANS AS THE POSTER FONT.
SO CHANTELLE GREEN FROM YEAR 10 BOUGHT
FIVE BAGS OF SKITTLES FROM COSTCUTTER.
I SAY TO HER 'CHANTELLE GREEN FROM YEAR 10
DID YOUS JUST BUY FIVE BAGS OF SKITTLES FROM
COSTCUTTER?'
CHANTELLE GREEN FROM YEAR 10 SAYS 'YEAH I
BOUGHT FIVE BAGS OF SKITTLES FROM
COSTCUTTER.'
I SAY 'BUT WHAT ABOUT YOUR DIABETES AND
SHIT?'
SHE LAUGHS.
I SAY 'ACTUALLY DIABETES IS A REALLY *SERIOUS
THING*. MY DAD HAS IT AND IT'S WELL HARSH!'
SHE'S PANICKIN NOW.
STARTS TO RUN AWAY.
PISSIN HERSELF SHE IS,
COS SHE KNOWS I'M BEHIND HER.
IT'S LITERALLY LIKE THE STAMPEDE SCENE IN *THE
LION KING*.
DON'T KNOW WHY I EVEN DID IT NOW.
I DON'T EVEN LIKE SKITTLES.
NOT-ALAN FROM YEAR 7,
I THOUGHT HIS NAME WAS ALAN BUT IT'S NOT
ALAN BUT I DON'T ACTUALLY KNOW WHAT HIS
NAME IS.
BUT NOT-ALAN FROM YEAR 7 SAYS SKITTLES GOT
REAL FRUIT IN THEM.
VITAMIN D AND SHIT.
SAYS THEY'RE HEALTHY FOR YOUS LIKE BREAD
AND BROCCOLI AND SOAP.
BUT WHEN SOMEONE DISRESPECTS YOUR FAMILY
YOUS GOTTA DO SOMETHIN ABOUT IT AIN'T YA?
I GOES UPS TO HER

GRABS HOLD OF ANYTHIN I CAN!
PULL!
PULL!
PUUUUUUULL!
I TRIED TO PULL HER HAIR OUT BUT I ONLY GOT
HER EXTENSIONS.
WHAT'S THAT?
CAN I KEEP IT?

SONNY. *Nhh-nhh*-nothin!

ROSHI. LEMME SEEEEEEEEEEEEEEEEEE!

SONNY. *P-P*-PISS OFF!

G-G-G-G–

ROSHI. MINE NOW!

SONNY (*desperately trying to say 'Give'*). *GI-GI-GI–*

ROSHI *playfully runs around with* SONNY*'s book. For her, it's the BEST GAME EVER.*

For SONNY*, this is torture.*

ROSHI. WHAT?
CAPTAIN CHATTER!!!!!
WHAT IS THIS!!!?

WAINWRIGHT *appears.*

WAINWRIGHT. OI YOU H̲ORMONAL DELINQUENT
DICKHEADS, GET IN HERE!

SONNY *snatches back his book.*

SONNY *and* ROSHI *enter* WAINWRIGHT*'s office.*

Her office is full of loads of eccentric stuff like a Lego Millennium Falcon *and a Pride flag.*

Piles of paper are also stacked up.

ROSHI. MISS, IS THAT YOUR WIFE IN THAT PHOTO?

WAINWRIGHT. I'm not engaging in that small talk.
Roshi, what did you do this time?

ROSHI. NOTHINNN MISS.

WAINWRIGHT. Well it says here
it said here
I just had it.
Why do people keep giving me more sheets of paper?
You pulled a girl's hair out?

ROSHI. NAH ONLY GOT HER EXTENSIONS.

WAINWRIGHT. Commiserations.
Better next luck time.
What about you New Boy?

SONNY. !!!

WAINWRIGHT. Twitchy boy, I'm talking to you.

SONNY. !!!

WAINWRIGHT. What's your name?

SONNY. *S-S-S-S-S-S-S-S-S-S-S–*

ROSHI. SANTA.

WAINWRIGHT. Shut up Roshi.
Take all the time you need.

SONNY. *S-S-S-S-S–*
*M-*my *nhhh-name I-I-I-I-I-I-*is –

An involuntary pause.

S-S-S-S-S-S–

AGHHHHHH!!

SONNY *closes his eyes and clenches his fists.*

*M-MMMH-MMMH-*MY *NHHH-NHHH-NHHH-name I-I-I-
I-I-I-I-I-I-I-I-*is –

SONNY *gets stuck in an even longer loop of repeating the
letter S.*

It feels like this is going to last for ETERNITY.

SONNY *looks to* WAINWRIGHT *pleadingly to ask
permission to stop speaking.*

WAINWRIGHT *shakes her head no.*

WAINWRIGHT. Everyone h̲as a name and I'd love to h̲ear yours.

SONNY. *S-S-S-S-S-… S-S-S-S-S-S-S-S-S-S-… S-S-S-S-S-S-S-S-S-S*-Sonny.

WAINWRIGHT. Thank you for telling me that. Sonny.
Right let's see
Sonny, cutting to the chase h̲ere, your behaviour today was possibly psychopathic.
Do you want to talk me through what h̲appened?

ROSHI. SERIOUSLY?

WAINWRIGHT. In your own time.
Take it away.
The floor is yours.

ROSHI. But he can't –

WAINWRIGHT (*to* ROSHI). THE FLOOR IS NEVER YOURS.
(*To* SONNY.) The floor is yours.

SONNY. This kid *CO-CO-CO*-comes up *T-T-T-TO M-M-M-M*-me –

WAINWRIGHT. So you stabbed h̲im in the eye with a fork?

ROSHI. SHITTTTTT!!

SONNY. *NHH-NHH-NHH-NHH-no n-N-N-no!*
It *WA-WA-WA-WA*-wasn't *LHH-LHH*-like that!

WAINWRIGHT. Well that's what it says h̲ere, Stabby McStab.
Anything else to say?

SONNY *shakes his head no.*

Nothing else to say?

SONNY *jumps up. He stops the action.*
He darts back and forth like a little rock star out of control.
He speaks at a frantic wild pace.
He is free.

SONNY. YES!
    IS THIS THE DEPUTY HEAD'S OFFICE?
    IT'S BEEN SHATTERED TO FAECES!
    SONNY SONNY SONNY!
    A B C D E F G H I J K L M N O P Q R S T U V W X Y Z
    I LIKE YOUR PENCILS, THEY LOOK POSH!
    DO YOUS LIKE *STAR WARS* MISS!? I LIKE *STAR WARS*
    MISS!
    MY NAME IS SONNY I LIKE DRAWIN AND WHEN I'M
    OLDER I'M GONNA BE AN ARTIST!
    I'M SORRY I GOT MAD AND THREW A FORK! I'M
    REALLY SORRY!
    SOMEONE HEAR ME.
    HEAR ME STARS.
    HEAR ME OCEANS.
    I FEEL LIKE I'M DISAPPEARIN.
    LIKE I'M FLOATIN AWAY.
    LIKE SOON THERE'LL BE NOTHIN LEFT.
    HELP ME! HELP ME! HELP ME! HELP! HELP ME!
    HELP ME!
    I'M HERE.
    HELLO?

WAINWRIGHT. Nothing else to say?
    No apology?
    Okay folks this is what's going to happen.
    I don't want to suspend anyone.
    So instead we're running a weekly lunchtime drama club.
    Yay.
    We need more members.
    Sonny there shouldn't be any forks there so you'll be fine.

SONNY. !!!
    !!

ROSHI. BUT IF IT'S AT LUNCH WHEN WILL WE EAT?
    WHEN WILL YOUS EAT?

WAINWRIGHT. I'm a teacher, I feed on the souls of bored
    schoolchildren.

SONNY *tries to leave*.

<u>H</u>old on Stabby McStab
Me and you are also going to be <u>h</u>aving awkward one-to-ones
so I can check you're not ripping the legs off spiders.

ROSHI. I DON'T WANNA HAVE ONE WITH YOUS!

WAINWRIGHT. I don't want to <u>h</u>ave one with you.

ROSHI. IS IT TRUE THE SCHOOL IS GONNA CLOSE
BECAUSE IT'S SHIT?

WAINWRIGHT. We can only pray.
Alright, get out of my office you little psychopaths.

WAINWRIGHT *disappears*.
SONNY *returns to the row of chairs outside the office*.
CAPTAIN CHATTER *appears*.

CAPTAIN CHATTER. HOLY ABDOMINAL AORTIC
ANEURYSM SONNY!
YOU CAN'T GO TO THIS LUNCHTIME DRAMA CLUB
TOMORROW!
SOMEONE ELSE MIGHT ASK YOU YOUR NAME!

SONNY. She said I need to go!

CAPTAIN CHATTER. HOLY LLANFAIRPWLL-
GWYNGYLLGOGERYCHWYRNDROB!
BUT YOUR ARCH ENEMIES VOWELS AND PUBLIC
SPEAKING WILL BE THERE!
STAY AT HOME!
SWEET SYRUPY SOLITUDE!

ROSHI *enters*.

ROSHI. LEFT MY GUM DIDN'T I.

CAPTAIN CHATTER. OHMYGOD A GIRL!
WANT ME TO KILL HER?

ROSHI *bends down and puts her hand under a chair and
searches for her gum*.

ROSHI. WANT SOME?

SONNY *is about to speak –*

CAPTAIN CHATTER. HOLY PAIN AU CHOCOLAT IF YOU
    SPEAK YOU WILL STAMMER!
    QUICKLY BACK TO THE HONEY-AND-LEMON
    SECRET SUPERHERO BASE!
    THERE ISN'T A SYLLABLE TO SPARE!
    WE CAN PLAN OPERATION COUGH COUGH I'M ILL
    AND CAN'T GO TO SCHOOL!
    IT'S NOT SAFE TO SPEAK FOR AT LEAST ANOTHER
    EIGHTY YEARS.

CAPTAIN CHATTER *flies away clutching* SONNY *tight.*

ROSHI *puts the gum in her mouth and chews for a bit.*

ROSHI. THIS TOTALLY ISN'T MY GUM.
    AH FUCK IT.

2

A school hall.
Lunchtime.

Everyone around SONNY *goes BLAH BLAH BLAH BLAH*
BLAH BLAH.
Maybe ROSHI *tries to talk to* SONNY *like BLAH BLAH BLAH*
BLAH BLAH BLAH but CAPTAIN CHATTER *isn't having*
<u>*ANY OF IT*</u>.

FISH. Welcome To Lunchtime Drama Club.
    Don't Think Of This As A *Punishment*, You Can Do
    Anything You Want Here. Jason Stop Doing That.
    I Thought It Would Be Super Fun If We Could Pass This
    Pillow Around And Each Say Something We Enjoy!
    I'm Miss Fish
    I'm Your New Headteacher.
    I Enjoy The Company Of My Cats, I Have Five And A Half.
    Pass It Along!

ROSHI. MY NAME'S ROSHI –

FISH. That's Enough.

A fluffy pillow begins to fly to SONNY. *It flies like a comet crashing to earth.*

SONNY *looks utterly terrified about speaking in public. The walls start to crack.*

CAPTAIN CHATTER. COMING AROUND THAT CIRCLE IS A PILLOW OF PURE FLUFFY EVIL!!!

SONNY. !!!!!!!!!!!!!!!!!!!!!!!!!!!!!!!!!!!!!!!

The pillow flies faster and faster. The ground shakes.

!!!!!!!!!!!!!!!!!!!!!!!!!!!!!!!!

The ceiling collapses.

CAPTAIN CHATTER. GET READY TO DEFLECT ON MY SIGNAL!!!!!!!!!

SONNY. !!
!!

The pillow lands in SONNY's *hands.*

CAPTAIN CHATTER. EVERYBODY'S LOOKING!!!!

A hundred eyeballs come out from the floorboards. The pillow also reveals it has eyes and stares at SONNY.

SONNY. !!
!!!
!!!

CAPTAIN CHATTER. JUST DON'T STAMMER!!!!!!

All the butterflies in the world enter his stomach. These lines should probably overlap. SONNY *opens his mouth.*

SONNY. MMM-MMMM –

CAPTAIN CHATTER. PASS IT OFF AS A COUGH! THE POWER OF A FAKE COUGH! SPLOOSH!

SONNY *coughs out laser beams.*

PRETEND YOU FORGOT THE QUESTION!
THE POWER OF DEFLECTION! BOOM!

SONNY. Ummmmmmmmmmmmmmmmmmm.

SONNY *stops time. Five. Four. Three. Two. One.*

MMM-MMMM-My name i-is S-S-S–

CAPTAIN CHATTER. OUCH! NOOOOOOO
THEY FOUND OUT YOU STAMMER!!!!!!!!!!!!!!!!!!!

The ceiling collapses even more.
CAPTAIN CHATTER *desperately holds it up trying to stop it from crushing them.*

SONNY. SHHHH-SHHHH –

CAPTAIN CHATTER. PLOP! NOOOOOO!
DON'T SAY YOUR NAME!
YOU ALWAYS STAMMER WHEN YOU SAY YOUR
NAME!
IT BEGINS WITH YOUR ARCH ENEMY THE LETTER S!

SONNY. I LLLLH-love A-A-A–

CAPTAIN CHATTER. OUCH! NOOOOOO!
YOU CAN'T SAY ART, REMEMBER!?
IT'S A TRAP FROM THE EVIL LEAGUE OF VOWELS!
SONNY YOU'RE SWEATING SO MUCH!

SONNY *sweats out a tsunami.*

NOOOO WHAT'S GOING ON WITH YOUR FACE!!?

SONNY *makes contorted faces. In his mind he's a grotesque creature.*
A handful of the letters fall from the sky.
SONNY *desperately tries to catch the falling words but they slip through his hands.*

SONNY *drowns in a sea of letters.*

```
A H I E U Z S H N D K Y H S A W U H I I L T O S U F V O S
O P R A V M B V U S K A Z C V H K L R Y O T T W K T N G
L O Y X O K A R W C V M R V A W Q N K L W P C I C T A L
R H I J O P I F J R Z E A R C T H U R N B Q M Y R I Q V Q N
Q F S T U J A N U B Q M H F Y O L R G I O I D M X V V A S
I V A E M K Z C R I U L U N C Z I T G D O N U J U L E I O P
F Q O W A L Z I H K E C M T Y Q U P C G P I K K F K K J X
M U H L R Z Y N G G X C C W D O G U I T Y X I F M H Q C
H T U J I W X J E S Q I X K F Z R Y R P O M H A H E L L L B
S M T C B D F G E X S M Q V Q A R T K U E I L Y X T G N I
M Z F F P J V Q T A I D A A M J E G A D S H V Q K O N Y S
C S F Y K O J V Y W K W O Q H O B R E K L I R M I W D C
D C V K X Y Z N N S N Q I R D O N C W J Y K O F V J R E S
L O Z R R A D T I L M X A K O E K D E G M I V U E R O N V
A M R Z G F D R U A A O T O G X Q B B V J P F D L N C J N
P Q H U W Z S H K Q E V H Y E W Z S H N D K Y H S G W U
H I Y L T O S K F V O S O P R A V M B V U S K Y Z C V H K
L R Y O T T W K T N G L O Y X O K R O W C V M R V W Q
N K L W P C I I C T A L R H J O P I F J R Z E R C T H U R N
B O Q M Y R Q V Q N Q F S T U J N U B Q M H F Y O L R G
I O D M X V V A S I V E M K Z C R U L U N C Z I T G D O N
U J U L E I O P F Q O W A L Z I H K E C M T Y Q U P C G P I
K K F K K J X M U H L R Z Y N G G X C C W D O G U I T Y
X I F M H Q C H T U J I W X J E S Q I X K F Z R Y R P O M
H A H E L L L B S M T C B 0 D F G E X S M Q V Q R T K U E
I L Y X T G N M Z F F P J V Q T A I D A A M J G A D S H V Q
K N Y S C S F Y K O J V Y W K W O Q H O B R E K L I R M
I W D C D C V K X Y Z N N S N Q I R D O N C W J Y K O F
V J R E S L O Z R R A D T I L M X A K E K D E G M I V U E
R O N V A M R Z G F D R U A A O E T O G X Q B B V J P F D
L N E C J N P Q H U W Z S H K Q E A I E V H Y E W Z S E H
N D K Y H S G W U H I Y L T O S K F V O S O P E R A V E M
B V U S K Y E Z C V H K L R Y O T T W K T N G L O Y E X
O K R E W C V I M R V W Q N K L W P C I I C T A L R H J O
P I F J R Z E R C T I H U R N B Q M I Y R E Q V Q I N Q F S
E T U J N U B Q M H F Y O L R G I O D M X V V A S I V E M
K Z C R U L I U N C Z I T G D O N E U J I U L E I O P F Q O
I W A L Z I H K E C M T Y E Q U P C G P I K K F K J X M U
H L R Z Y N G G X C C W D O G U I T Y X I F M H Q C H T
```

```
UJIWSXJESQAIXKFZRYREPOMHAHSELL
LBSMTAZCBDFGEXSMQVQRTKUEILYXT
GNMZFFPJVQTAIDAAMJGADSHVQKNYS
CSFYKOJVYWKWOQHOBREKLIRMIWDC
DCVKXYZNNSNQIRDONCWJYKOFVJRES
LOZRRADTILMXAKEKDEGMIVUERONVA
MRZGFDRUAAOTOGXQBBVJPFDLNCJNP
QHUWZSHKQEVHYEWZSHNDKYHSGWUH
IYLTOSKFVOSOPRAVMBVUSKYZCVHKL
RYOTTWKTNGLOYXOKRWCVMRVWQNK
LWPCIICTALRHJOPIFJRZERCTHURNBQ
MYRQVQNQFSTUJNUBQMHFYOLRGIOD
MXVVASIVEMKZCRULUNCZITGDONUJU
LEIOPFQOWALZIHKECMTYQUPCGPIKKF
KKJXMUHLRZYNGGXCCWDOGUITYXIF
MHQCHTUJIWXJESQIXKFZRYRPOMHAH
ELLLBSMTCBDFGEXSMQVQRTKUEILYX
TGNMZFFPJVQTAIDAAMJGADSHVQKNY
SCSFYKOJVYWKWOQHOBREKLIRMIWD
CDCVKXYZNNSNQIRDONCWJYKOFVJRE
SLOZRRADTILMXAKEKDEGMIVUERONV
AMRZGFDRUAAOTOGXQBBVJPFDLNCJN
PQHUWZSHKQEVHYEWZSHNDKYHSGWU
HIYLTOSKFVOSOPRAVMBVUSKYZCVHK
LRYOTTWKTNGLOYXOKRWCVMRVWQN
KLWPCIICTALRHJOPIFJRZERCTHURNB
QMYRQVQNQFSTUJNUBQMHFYOLRGIO
DMXVVASIVEMKZCRULUNCZITGDONUJ
ULEIOPFQOWALZIHKECMTYQUPCGPIKK
FKKJXMUHLRZYNGGXCCWDOGUITYXIF
MHQCHTUJIWXJESQIXKFZRYRPOMHAH
ELLLBSMTCBDFGEXSMQVQRTKUEILYX
TGNMZFFPJVQTAIDAAMJGADSHVQKNY
SCSFYKOJVYWKWOQHOBREKLIRMIWD
CDCVKXYZNNSNQIRDONCWJYKOFVJRE
SLOZRRADTILMXAKEKDEGMIVUERONV
AMRZGFDRUAAOTOGXQBBVJPFDLNCJN
PQHUWZSHKQEVHYEWZSHNDKYHSGWU
HIYLTOSKFVOSOPRQCPMVOXCXTQOYZ
```

```
V P R T E G C K Q M I J D O X A M Z E W K H A E Z I L L M
Z K Y A P C A N F O C L X B Z M H C X T Q O Y Z V P R T E
G C K Q M I J D O X A M Z E W K H A E Z I L L M Z K Y A P
C A N F O C L X B Z M H C P V O N O P X Z R I Y M P N K S
L R A O W Y L U T C D I A N Y J X O L R Q S Y P O P K J P E
B W W U E Q B Z D F T E V V F F E B C P M T C W S P G L
L Z R J N E D R X O Z J U L Q J T N U X I Z P G J R R G P J F
X K O A L O Q W O J R X L D E L K I O E U D B Z K Y W B
F I Z E L D H A H U D J Q Y H L H D O Z E R G W N V X V S
K N U N A H P M W M S S V T C M J G X L D R Q U U S B T
J R W R Q L N V D E R E P A E G E J L Q T J H Y A N J X C Q
I S Z C P B H A I A C E I N E D H E W E R T L S A Y N J W X
C T R V N G Q P G T S F P K F N Q Q G U E Q O A U M C W
G B H V G U A Y B F I U A X Y F U G C T I Q T J Q R W D V
Z K L R J U R S G N S N N U T I G H R C T P K Y A V Y L P X
L G R P R U W Z B T N M F W N V X E T E C K M O OO I H
G Y O A T Q E V T Y D E D H L R D T D J K G I A Q N S W J
D S Y D F D T T C R A E P K L E X H W U E V A L W S E K K
O B N L C R B L M I V H J R L B Y P X H H W Y Q T V N U J
E X T D S U Z V N F W M F G W C Y O U N Q V Y G H V Y M
D P E X E F K B Z Z J G P N U O Q S D R R N I O W A U L J
T F T K E M F A K D D R S F I N T H I J V S G N N P X C L V
C I X J K D J G T Y W L D R O X V V Q R M W R F C U D G
N T D Q R A L T M M N E M F W T G F Z L Z T B B Y M E M
D U U S C D Z Y H I F D I D E E Y V I A Z U S J L U N Y M C
X U M J T J F C S D J G J F O P K G F M B S T P E L R Z C N
V A G S N M T M M W C H M Y F T F A L V A Z L Z R V S N
C P S G R P N N Z N D A H V Z H H C S Y I V H X F J W V I
Q M W L D T T E M J H U Q H P S X X S N E T H H W R G Z
E M A Q L D T Q O Z U R B A K Q U F M O U J Y S L V K O
O L O K M N I M A E P H B Z U L I K S M F L Q Q U Y U S Q
W Y Z V Z G F F M M E E T P U K E G W Z E V G V U O Q B
P C T X T V Z Y Z N F X D B D E S D K E S V X L Z U U U V
L D N W Y H J W K R C C C J A T K P E E P T O S A J V A Z R
X T J P G Y O G S D K B P J X K S S N Z B H R Y J Y V J X V
V A S I V E M K Z C R U L U N C Z I T G D O N U J U L E I O
P F Q O W A L Z I H K E C M T Y Q U P C G P I K K F K K J
X M U H L R Z Y N G G X C C W D O G U I T Y X I F M H Q
C H T U J I W X J E S Q I X K F Z R Y R P O M H A H E L L L
```

B S M T C B D F G E X S M Q V Q R T K U E I L Y X T G N
M Z F F P J V Q T A I D A A M J G A D S H V Q K N Y S C S F
Y K O J V Y W K W O Q H O B R E K L I R M I W D C D C V
K X Y Z N N S N Q I R D O N C W J Y K O F V J R E I O S L
O Z R R A D T I L M X A K E K D E G M I V U E R O N V A
M R Z G F D R U A A O T O G X Q B B V J P F D L N C J N P
Q H U W Z S H K Q E E I T G J Y T F I R E K V H J Y E W Z S
H N D K Y H S G W U H I Y L T O S K F V O S O P R I G H R
C T P K Y A V Y L P X L G R P R U W Z B T N M F W N V Q U
P C G P I K K F K K J X M U H L R Z Y N G G X C C W D O
G U I T Y X I F M H Q C H T U J I W X J E S Q I A F E Y S G
K A D F G H E I I E S F P O G R F G H C G K D H D E R T P
O R T S T Y P D H R A J L D R O P O I U Y T R U H D B D E
G S V J I O P U T G E D F E A C F I R T F E W A C T F G R W
O P R F T J D F U G T D K G T R D K I E D T G R E W Q A C
P T G F U F R T W J D L I T E F K R W R U R F D J G T E Q P
D T S J I T F R E R T O F G D J U T R K T U R E I F D R T Y U
C G H R E W O G F P R T F E T S O F J E G B E U G E A U I F
T D H F T S A K I E C O M U T F Y I Q T U E P I C O G U P
S I K O U F G T R W E R F H G T Y F W I D G C I L E X O B
U Z E M E H I C O X U T E Q E O E Y T Z O V U P E R O T
W E R G T C I K U Q U M I J D O X A M Z E W K H A E Z I L
L M Z K Y A P C A N F O C L X B Z M H C P V O N O P X Z
R I Y M P N K S L R A H D O R T Y F K R I O T F G U R D F
G R E O F E O F E H I T S T O T S J T S O T I I I O T E F G H
I T O G R S L G R G H I K T D L G T O T U G T U D T U G L
G H T R U R W I G D I G T I E I O U R A H H S R T F I E F G
R I F R I D E O D F R I D G T S H I T G T D O T S I T R K G T
R O I R G T O E I R F R U G R S U T R U E T O S E G I R W
I D E D P Q E T G J D F R U R W R K F E T I L D J W T R F U
F G T P C A Q W E R G T D E I K D R T G K D T G F F P J V
Q T A I D A A M J G P J V Q T A I D A A M J G P J V Q T A I D
A A M J G N Y S C S F Y K O J V Y W K W O Q H O B R E K
L I R M I W D C D C V K X Y Z N N S N Q I R D O N C W J Y
K O F V J R E S L O Z R R A D T I L M X A K E K D E G M I
V U E R O N V A M R Z G F D R U A A O T O G X Q B B V J
P F D L N C J N P Q H U W Z S H K Q E T F I E E T D J D I O
E V H J Y E W Z S H N D K Y H S G W U H I Y L T O S K
F V O S O P R I G H R C T P K Y A V Y L P X L G R P R U W

SONNY *isn't giving up.*
He tries to catch the letters but CAPTAIN CHATTER *holds him back.*
A single word 'SONNY' slowly falls.
SONNY *sadly watches his name fall.*
The word lands on the ground.
SONNY s*tomps on it.*
He stomps on it again.
And again.
And again.
His rage grows.
He throws the pillow on the ground and runs out of the hall.

3

WAINWRIGHT*'s office.*
After school.

SONNY *is sitting in silence looking down at the floor.*
His hands subconsciously play with a pencil set on the desk.

WAINWRIGHT. This is fun.

> WAINWRIGHT *begins to fold* SONNY*'s report into a paper plane.*
> *She finishes it and throws it across the office to him.*

(*As it flies across the room.*) I can't wait for our holiday –
(*As the paper plane falls she makes sounds of explosions.*)
Noooooooooo why did we catch this paper plane instead of British Airways!?

> SONNY *slowly looks up.*
> *His eyes dart around* WAINWRIGHT*'s desk.*
> *He picks up the pencil set lightly and stares at it in amazement.*

You like that pencil set?
You keep eyeballing it like – (*Does an impression.*)

He quickly shakes his head no.

It was a Secret Santa.
That and the soap.
You can have them if you want?
The soap smells like arse.

SONNY *pushes the pencil set away and crosses his arms.*
He goes back to staring at the floor.
He picks up the soap and smells it.
It does smell like arse.

Told you.

Realising SONNY *might start a conversation*
CAPTIAN CHATTER *throws the pencil set and soap*
straight into the sun.

How is the new foster placement going?
Good?

SONNY....

WAINWRIGHT. If we're just going to sit in silence you don't
mind if I eat some food do you?

WAINWRIGHT *takes out some Ryvita, puts salmon and*
avocado on top and eats it.

SONNY *slowly looks up and stares at the Ryvita.*

Ryvita. Want some?

SONNY *shakes his head no.*
He wants to ask a question.
He wants to ask a question.
Fuck it. He's going to ask the question.
HERE HE GOES! HERE HE GOES! HERE HE GOES!

SONNY. *WH-WH– t-t-the hell is t-t-that Miss?*

WAINWRIGHT. It's basically shit bread.

WAINWRIGHT *waves it in* SONNY*'s face.*

SONNY *is grossed out by it.*

What food do you like Stabby McStab?

SONNY *shrugs his shoulders and looks to the floor.*

But actually that Speaking Thing was fun.

SONNY. *M-M-M-M*-Miss *w-w-w*-where *d-d-d*-do *y-y*-you *s-s*-shop?

WAINWRIGHT....

SONNY....

WAINWRIGHT. Waitrose.

SONNY. WHAAAAAAAT!!!!!!!! *WHH*–WAITROSE *WHH-WA-WA-WA*-WANKER!!!!

WAINWRIGHT. That's me.

SONNY. *M-M-M-MISS, Y-Y-Y*-YO-*E-E-E*-EAT *S-S-SHH*-STUFF LIKE *C-C-C-C*-CAVIAR?

WAINWRIGHT. Tried it once, too salty.

SONNY. EWWWWWWWWWWWWWWWWW!

WAINWRIGHT. What!?

SONNY. *Y-Y*-YOU *A-A-A-A*-ATE *F-F-F-F-F*-SHH-SHH-SHH-SHH-SHIT!

WAINWRIGHT. No I ate fish eggs.

SONNY. *N-N*-NAH *N-M-M-M*-MISS –
(*An involuntary pause on the letter 'I'.*)
IT'S *F*-FISH SHH-SHH-SHH SHIT
DID YOU SUCK IT DIRECTLY FROM THE FISH'S ASS?

WAINWRIGHT. So do you –

SONNY. OHMYGOD YOU DID MISS!!!!!!! YOU
DID!!!!!!!!!!!!!!!
M-MISS YHH-YHH-YOUS FIGHT IN THE *S-S-SH-SH*-SECOND *W-W*-WORLD *W*-WAR?

WAINWRIGHT. Yes I shot Hitler.
So Stabby McStab
you've successfully avoided telling me anything about yourself.

Congratulations, your prize is that you get to tell me
something about yourself!
What is it you like? No scratch that.
What is it you *love*?
Sorry I just spat Ryvita at you.

SONNY *sits up higher and higher and higher into the chair.*
Now at the same level as WAINWRIGHT.
Ready to speak.
Ready to finally tell someone what he loves.
He opens his mouth.
He remembers.
There are words and letters everywhere.
He slowly shrinks back into the chair.

SONNY. *N-n*-nothin.

WAINWRIGHT. You're boring.
You must love something?
If you don't tell me I will tell you all the boring shit I like.

SONNY. I li-*l-l-l*-love – (*Trying to say 'art'.*)
a-a-a–

SONNY *slams his fists on the desk.*

WAINWRIGHT. Hitting my table? I love doing that as well.

SONNY (*an involuntary pause on the word 'I'*). I love *a-a-a-a-*
a–
(*An involuntary pause on the word 'I'.*)
I *d-d*-does *l-l-l-l-l*-love *t*-things!

WAINWRIGHT. I know
So go ahead, tell me.

SONNY *mouths the words 'I love' over and over again.*

SONNY (*with all the will in the universe*). A-A-A-A-ART!

WAINWRIGHT. Art?

SONNY *enthusiastically nods and nods and nods.*
Right now he could nod for hours.

Visiting galleries or drawing?

SONNY *sits up. Suddenly this conversation has got a lot more enjoyable.*

SONNY (*trying to say 'Drawing'*). *D-D-D-D-D–*
(*Trying to say 'Drawing'.*) *D-D-D-D-D–*
(*Trying to say 'Drawing'.*) *D-D-D-D-D–*
UGH!

SONNY *draws her a picture.*

WAINWRIGHT. Bloody <u>h</u>ell!
These are great.
You're an artist who moonlights as a violent kid.
Jesus I keep spitting Ryvita at you, I'm so sorry.
We need to fill out this form,
it's the reason for these awkward meetings.
This is another new scheme created by our *enthusiastic* new headteacher.
It's called the 'behaviour development solution scheme'.
It's a series of weekly questions.
'Name of *problem child.*'
Very sensitive.
Jesus Christ there's thirty questions!
Get your game face on Stabby McStab.
Number one. Yes or no?
'*I* feel confident when I am requested to perform a task'?

SONNY. Uhhh –

WAINWRIGHT. Stupid question.
You're twelve, you wouldn't <u>h</u>ave felt an ounce of confidence yet. So big fat *no* right?
Two. 'I sometimes or often struggle with techniques that my peers find easy?'

SONNY. *S-S-S-S-S-S-S-S-*Sometimes *w-w-*when –

WAINWRIGHT. Just a yes or no kid.
The form doesn't actually care what you struggle with it just wants to know if you struggle.
Is that a yes?

SONNY *nods yes.*

'*I lack the clarity, courage, and determination to exceed in an academic environment.*'
Wow that is the worst sentence ever written.
Enough.

WAINWRIGHT *folds the form into another paper plane and flies it across to* SONNY.

Let's speak about your least favourite subject again, you.

SONNY. !!!

WAINWRIGHT. Are you <u>h</u>appy in your new placement?
What's her name again?

SONNY. J-J-J-J-J-Jackie –

WAINWRIGHT. What does Jackie do?

SONNY *shrugs his shoulders.*

Well Jackie sounds real interesting.
Do you speak to her much?

SONNY. *D-d-d-d-d-*don't *shh-shh-shh-*speak Miss.

WAINWRIGHT. That's a shame because I think you're a pretty great communicator.

Fake News, thinks CAPTAIN CHATTER.

You know there's nothing wrong with stammering right?

CAPTAIN CHATTER *guffaws at this.*

SONNY *holds the plane in his hand unsure whether to fly it back.*

SONNY....

WAINWRIGHT. Okay you're staring at me.
Are you staring at my <u>h</u>air?
If you're staring at my <u>h</u>air I just want you to know I used some new <u>H</u>ead & Shoulders shampoo and it's made my <u>h</u>air very poofy and I'm very insecure about it.

SONNY. *N-n-n-*no *ahh-ahh-ahh-ahh-e-e-*ever *s-s-*said that before.

WAINWRIGHT. Shouldn't have said the hair thing.
Why did I say the hair thing?

SONNY *flies the plane back*.

How does stammering make you feel Sonny?

WAINWRIGHT *flies the plane back*.

SONNY *stops the action*.

SONNY. It's like everyone else is flyin and I'm just standin still.
But I wanna fly.
I wanna soar.

CAPTAIN CHATTER. HOW ARE YOU EVER GOING TO GET A JOB?
HOW ARE YOU EVER GOING TO MEET A PARTNER?

SONNY. I wanna *soar*!

CAPTAIN CHATTER. AFRAID OF YOUR OWN NAME.

SONNY. I wanna *soar*!

CAPTAIN CHATTER. WHAT USE IS A BOY WHO CAN'T SAY HIS OWN NAME?

SONNY. I WANNA *SOAR*!

CAPTAIN CHATTER. *'MAKE A GOOD FIRST IMPRESSION SONNY!'*
COULDN'T EVEN INTRODUCE YOURSELF TO POTENTIAL FOSTER PARENTS.
'THIS IS SONNY, HE'S ONE OF OUR SPECIAL BOYS'
THERE'S NOTHING SPECIAL ABOUT NOT BEING ABLE TO SPEAK!

SONNY. I WANNA *SOAR*!

CAPTAIN CHATTER. RING RING!
'ANSWER THE PHONE SONNY, IT'S JUST A PHONE.'
'YOU'RE NOT SCARED OF A PHONE ARE YOU?'

SONNY. I WANNA SOAR!

CAPTAIN CHATTER. *'IF YOU NEED THE TOILET JUST
PUT YOUR HAND UP AND ASK.'*
*'MISS, I THINK SONNY'S PISSED HIMSELF!
HAAAAAAAAAAAAAAA!'*

SONNY (*at the top of his lungs*). I WANNA SOAR!

CAPTAIN CHATTER. *'OPEN THE DOOR MUM! MUM!?
MUMMY!?'*
SHE WON'T W-W-W-W-W-WAKE U-U-U-U-U-P!!!'

SONNY *opens his mouth ready to speak.
He slowly crushes the paper plane in his hands.
He runs out of the office.*

WAINWRIGHT. See you next week Sonny.

4

*The lockers.
After school.*

SONNY *sits drawing alone.*

ROSHI *bursts out of a locker making* SONNY *SHIT HIMSELF.*

ROSHI. I FOUND A DEAD BIRD.
WANNA COME POKE IT WITH A STICK?

NOT-ALAN I'M GOIN TO POKE THE DEAD BIRD
AGAIN!!!!!!!

NOT-ALAN IT IS A WORK THING!!!!!!!

THAT'S MY OFFICE. I RUN A BUISINESS.

I SAID OUR OFFICE NOT-ALAN!!!

THAT'S MY OFFICE. I RUN A BUSINESS.

WE'RE TRYIN TO SELL NOT-ALAN'S RETAINER SO
WE CAN BUY A LAMBORGHINI BUT NOT-ALAN

KEEPS THREATENIN TO LIQUIFY HIS ASSETS
BECAUSE NOT-ALAN'S MUM GROUNDED HIM.
LIKE LITERALLY EVER SINCE NOT-ALAN'S MUM
GOT THAT JOB IN SPAR SHE ACTS LIKE SHE'S
EAMONN HOLMES.

NOT-ALAN I CAN HEAR YOUS BREATHIN THROUGH
THE VENTS.
REMEMBER WHAT I SAID NOT-ALAN IF YOU'RE
BREATHIN YOU'RE NOT SELLIN!!
THE VENTS ARE FOR ME.

COME POKE THE BIRD SONNY?
IT'S A VERY SQUISHY BIRD SONNY!

SONNY. I saw yous yesterday!

ROSHI. I'M GONNA HOLD MY BREATH UNTIL YOUS
POKE THE BIRD WITH ME AND THEN WHEN I DIE
IT'S GONNA BE YOUR FAULT.

SONNY. Fineeeeeeee!

ROSHI. I STOLE SOME DOUGHNUTS FROM GREGGS
AND WAS LIKE TO THE MANAGER IF YOUS TOUCH
ME I WILL SCREAM
AND ONCE THAT SCREAM HAS LEFT MY MOUTH I
WILL TEAR YOUR GUTS OUT.
MMM CHOCOLATE!!
I THOUGHT NOW THAT I DECIDED WE'RE BEST
FRIENDS I'D GIVE SOME TO YOUS.
CATCH!

ROSHI *throws a doughnut to* SONNY.

He fails to catch it and it lands on the floor.

HEY I CAN FIT AN ENTIRE GREGGS DOUGHNUT IN
MY MOUTH
WANNA SEE?

SONNY. *Nhh-nhh-nhh-*no yous can't.

ROSHI. YEAH I CAN. WANNA SEE?

SONNY. Y-y-y-yeah.

SONNY *picks up the doughnut and eats it.*

SONNY'S MUM *appears.*

ROSHI. SONNY YOUS WATCHIN?

SONNY'S MUM. It's been on the floor!

SONNY. Muuuuuuuum five-second rule!

SONNY'S MUM. That's not a thing!

ROSHI. SONNY YOUS WATCHIN?

SONNY *runs to his* MUM *and playfully tries to make her eat it*

SONNY'S MUM. EUCK! That's it run!

SONNY'S MUM *playfully chases* SONNY.

She ruffles his hair. SONNY *giggles.*

If yous could have spoken it would have been like this all the time.

SONNY*'s soul rots.*

5

WAINWRIGHT*'s office.*
WAINWRIGHT *is doing fuck-all.*
ROSHI *comes running in.*

WAINWRIGHT. I'm really busy.

ROSHI. COME WITH!

ROSHI *grabs* WAINWRIGHT *and runs into the hallway.*

SONNY *is punching the row of chairs, lost in a world of rage and violence.*
His knuckles are dripping blood.

MISS, WANTS ME TO GET WHOEVER'S ON
TIMEOUT?

WAINWRIGHT. That won't solve the problem
just lock the problem in a confined space.
Sonny, what's wrong?

SONNY'S MUM. Don't come in. No no I'm fine. Just don't
come in!

SONNY *punches the chair with a mighty fury.*
This fury makes WAINWRIGHT *step back with fear.*
SONNY *punches harder and harder.*

*Th-th-th-th-th-th-*they TOOK *I-I-I-*IT.

WAINWRIGHT. What did they take?

SONNY. *Mmmm-mmmm-mmm-MMMM–* C-C-COMIC!

ROSHI. Who?

SONNY (*an involuntary pause on the word 'Aaron'*).
(*Another involuntary pause on the word 'Aaron'.*)
(*And another involuntary pause on the word 'Aaron'.*)
*A-A-A-A-A-A-A-*AARON *S-S-S-*SMITH!
Thhh-thh-thh-took –
(*An involuntary pause on the word 'it'.*) it
*frh-frh-frh-frh-*from
*mmmmh-mmmmmmh-*my *bhh-bhhh-bhh-*bag *ahh-ahh-ahh-*
*ahh-ahh-ahh-ahh-*AND –

He doesn't speak.
Not because he can't. But because he can't bring himself to
say the following sentence.

S-S-S-S-S–

SONNY *begins punching the chair, with each punch*
growing faster, harder and more hateful.

S-S-S-S-S– (*With a mighty rage.*) SHITS *OHH-O-O-O-*ON
IT!

ROSHI. I'LL KILL HIM!

WAINWRIGHT. Let me <u>h</u>andle this.

ROSHI *exits*.

Roshi! Oh god!
Uhhh Sonny get in the office!
What comic book?
If you don't *tell me*, I can't <u>h</u>elp you.

ROSHI *slowly returns. She has a bits of paper in her hands*.

ROSHI. Uhhhh Sonny, they must have ripped it after...
y'know...
i tried to get more but, this was all that wasn't covered in...
y'know...

She gently places the pieces in SONNY*'s hands*.
SONNY *lets the pieces fall around him*.

Sorry, Sonny.

WAINWRIGHT. I'll just get you a new book.

SONNY. *N-n-n-n*-no –

WAINWRIGHT. <u>H</u>ave it. Actually, you can <u>h</u>ave two.

SONNY. *N-N-N-N-NO!*
D-d-d-don't *g-g-g*-get *i-i-i*-it!

WAINWRIGHT. Well *tell me* then!?

SONNY (*an involuntary pause on the word 'I'*). *I-I-I-I-I-CHH-
CHH-CHH-CHH-CHH CA-CA-CA-CA-CA*-CAN'T
T-T-T-T-TELL *YH-YH-YH-YH-YH*-UGHH!

WAINWRIGHT. We'll get you another one.

WAINWRIGHT *tries to pick up the pieces*.
SONNY *desperately tries to keep them*.

If it's been near what you say it has, I don't want it in my
office.

SONNY. *N-N-N-N-N*-NO!

WAINWRIGHT. Sonny –

SONNY. *N-N-N-N-N*-NO!

WAINWRIGHT. Give it to me, yuck!

SONNY. *NHH-NHH-NHH-NHH-NHH – NHH NHH-NHH –*

In the struggle SONNY *strikes* WAINWRIGHT *on the nose.*
SONNY stares at his hand terrified of what he's just done.
He then tries to walk to WAINWRIGHT.

WAINWRIGHT. Stay away!

(*Regains teacher self.*) No, stay there, please.

Just stay there.

So thanks for your help Roshi, this has been fun.

ROSHI. WANNA BUY NOT-ALAN'S RETAINER?

WAINWRIGHT *ushers* ROSHI *out of the office.*

SONNY *looks to the floor.*
He tries to say sorry but gets stuck in an involuntary pause.

WAINWRIGHT. Sonny.
I'm going to <u>h</u>ave to –

She can't bring herself to say it.

SONNY *points to his mouth.*

I'm going to <u>h</u>ave to ask you to…

Hell, I don't know what was in that book of yours.
But I do know whatever it was, you *truly loved* it
and when it comes to the things we love, we make stupid
decisions.

SONNY *tries to stop himself crying but today it won't stop.*

Are you okay?

Suddenly his crying is set free.
He clenches his fists with anger.

Oh come on now. No need for that. Tell me what's wrong,
come on?

With each new falling tear SONNY *starts softly punching the floor.*

Tell me what's wrong?

SONNY *points to his mouth and shakes his head.*
The crying continues.
The floor punching continues.
Words are useless now.

I'm not allowed to <u>h</u>ug you.
Our new school policy says I'm not allowed to <u>h</u>ug you.

WAINWRIGHT *walks over to* SONNY *longing to hug him.*

I'm not allowed to <u>h</u>ug you...

WAINWRIGHT *stands over a crying* SONNY, *looking demoralised, feeling useless and redundant.*

I'll get some Sellotape for those pieces...

SONNY*'s soul rots.*

6

School hall.
Lunchtime.

SONNY *looks lonelier than ever.*
A group of students play freely with words HELLO.
SONNY *looks around for help. He points to his mouth. He pleads for help. No one notices.*
SONNY *brings out a knife.*
He cuts out his vocal cords and throws them on the floor.
CAPTAIN CHATTER *proudly wears them like a Gucci accessory.*

7

WAINWRIGHT's *office.*
After school.

SONNY *gives a smile to* WAINWRIGHT. *She doesn't smile back.*
CAPTAIN CHATTER *is flossing with* SONNY's *vocal cords or some mad shit like that.*

WAINWRIGHT. Sit.

I said sit.

Don't touch my shit.

SONNY *looks sad.*
He holds his stomach showing signs of starvation.

Right, Behaviour Development Scheme.
Question number one…

SONNY *makes a paper plane and flies it across the office to her.*
He laughs.
She doesn't.

Stop.

'In the past week, I felt confident when I was requested to perform a task'?

SONNY *holds his stomach in pain.*
He stares at the Ryvita.

Are you –

(Reverting back to formal teacher mode.) *'In the past week I felt confident when I was requested to perform a task'?*
'In the past week I felt – ' *(A pause.)* What's wrong?

SONNY. *Nhh-nhh-nhh –*

WAINWRIGHT. Zombie Sonny, what's wrong?

SONNY. *H-h-h-*hungry.

WAINWRIGHT. What did you <u>h</u>ave for lunch?

SONNY. *B-b*-biscuits.

WAINWRIGHT. Nutritional. Why?

SONNY. I *l-l*-like *e-e-e*-em!

WAINWRIGHT. Yeah but not for lunch you weirdo.

You need to *ask* for the food you want from the canteen don't you?

SONNY....

WAINWRIGHT. <u>H</u>ave some Ryvita?

SONNY. Miss – (*An involuntary pause on the word 'I'*.) I, w*a-wa*-wanna *shh-s-s-shh-shh-shh*-say... *f-f-f*-yesterday. (*Attempts to say 'Sorry'*.) *S-s-s-s-s-s-s*–

WAINWRIGHT. Sonny, it's fine.
Eat.

SONNY (*that bit more desperate*). *S-s-s-s-s-s-s!*

WAINWRIGHT. I know.

FISH *barges through the door.*

FISH (*speaking over* SONNY). HERE HE IS, MR CELEBRITY!

SONNY (*spoken over by* FISH). *S*-sorry.

WAINWRIGHT. I <u>h</u>aven't told him yet.
I was about to.

FISH. Let me tell him.

WAINWRIGHT. Please, he doesn't know.

FISH. I'll tell him *very sensitively*. Let me tell him.

WAINWRIGHT. Not like this.

FISH. YOU'VE GOT A LINE IN THE SCHOOL PLAY!

SONNY. !!
!!!

SONNY *is terrified and motionless.*
The walls close in.

FISH. YOU'RE PLAYING A GUARD IN *HAMLET*!

SONNY. !!!!!!!!!!!!!!!!!!!!!!!!!!!!!!!!!!!!!!
!!
!!

The walls close in even more. Getting closer and closer and closer.

FISH. AND YOU'LL GET TO SAY YOUR LINES IN
PUBLIC!

SONNY. !!!!!!!!!!!!!!!!!!!!!!!!!!!!!!!!!!!!!!
!!
!!
!!!

The walls continue to close in almost crushing SONNY.
He struggles to breathe.

FISH. Can I Have Your Autograph Mr Actor!?
Just A Joke I Don't Really Want Your Autograph Because
You're Not Famous.

WAINWRIGHT. Sonny, are you okay?

FISH. He's completely fine.

Suddenly FISH *reveals a GIANT FUCKING KNIFE!!!!!*

ARE YOU READY TO DIE YOU MOTHERFUCKER!?
IT'S GOING TO BE LONG AND SLOW! JUST THE WAY
I LIKE IT!!!

She licks her knife in an animalistic way and then licks
SONNY's *face.*

THE BARD IS COMING!
THE BARD IS COMING!
THE BARD IS COMING!
MWHAHAHAHAHAHAHAHA!!!

I mean it's only saying a few silly lines.
Nobody gets left behind in my school. Has anyone seen Jason?

WAINWRIGHT. Miss Fish wait.
You spoke over Sonny earlier.
Never do that again.
Understand?

FISH *isn't sure if she should retaliate or not.*
Maybe she's doing some BIG TIME mouth breathing.
Probably planning to strangle her in her sleep or something.
She leaves.

I'm sorry lovely.
I wanted to be the one to tell you.

SONNY. !!!

WAINWRIGHT. You're not <u>h</u>aving a stroke are you?
Nod if you're <u>h</u>aving a stroke?

SONNY. *Y-y-y–* you *chh-*can get *m-m-m-m-*me out of *i-i-i-i-*it yeah?

WAINWRIGHT. It's out of my <u>h</u>ands –

SONNY. *P-P-P-P-P-*PLEASE!
(*An involuntary pause on the word 'I'll'.*) I'll *m-m-m-m-m-*move!

WAINWRIGHT. And what will you do the *next time* you're made to *speak*?

SONNY. *M-m-*move!

WAINWRIGHT. And the next time?

SONNY. *M-m-*move!

WAINWRIGHT. This is going to cost you a fortune in moving fees.
It's one scene.

CAPTAIN CHATTER. THE BARD IS COMING –

WAINWRIGHT. One tiny scene.

CAPTAIN CHATTER. THE BARD IS COMING –

WAINWRIGHT. Who gives a shit if you stammer –

CAPTAIN CHATTER. THE BARD IS COMING –

WAINWRIGHT. I can help you learn the lines –

CAPTAIN CHATTER. THE BARD IS COMING –

WAINWRIGHT. And there's techniques –

CAPTAIN CHATTER. THE BARD IS COMING –

WAINWRIGHT. More relaxed ways of speaking –

CAPTAIN CHATTER. THE BARD IS COMING –

WAINWRIGHT. I can help you?

CAPTAIN CHATTER. THE BARD IS COMINGGGGG!

FUCKING HELL!!!!!!!!!!!!!!!!!!!!!!!!!!!!!!!!!!

A GIANT DERANGED DEMONIC WILLIAM SHAKESPEARE SLOWLY RISES FROM OUT THE FLOORBOARDS.

SONNY. !!!
!!
!!
!!
!!
!!
!!
!!
!!
!!
!!
!!
!!
!!
!!
!!

!!
!!
!!
!!
!!
!!
!!
!!
!!
!!
!!
!!
!!
!!
!!
!!
!!
!!
!!
!!
!!
!!
!!
!!
!!
!!
!!
!!
!!
!!
!!
!!
!!
!!
!!
!!
!!
!!
!!

!!
!!
!!
!!
!!
!!
!!

WILLIAM SHAKESPEARE *sets* WAINWRIGHT's *office
on fire.*
What once felt like a safe place is utterly destroyed.
WILLIAM SHAKESPEARE *lets out a mighty deafening
screech.*
Doom is coming.

8

The lockers.
After school.

SONNY *runs in.*
No one's here. Thank fuck. All safe, all good.
ROSHI *jumps from out from a locker terrifying him.*
She's holding a skull.
She's dressed in FULL-ON ye olde Shakespearean gear.

ROSHI. THIS BITCH IS PLAYIN HAMLET!!!

NOT-ALAN YOUS WERE MEANT TO PLAY MY
ENTRANCE MUSIC!!!!!!!

NOT-ALAN HAVE YOUS PASSED OUT AGAIN?

SONNY. Whh-whh-whh-when did yous get in!?

ROSHI. I'VE BEEN WAITIN HERE ALL AFTERNOON FOR
YOUS.
HAD TO GO HOME TO GET MY DOG'S SKULL FIRST.
THIS BITCH IS PLAYIN HAMLET!!!

SONNY. I'm not doin a shitty play about ham!

ROSHI. NOT-ALAN WAS CAST AS HAMLET BUT HE
SWAPPED IT FOR A TOFFEE CRISP.

SONNY. Whh-whh-whh-what the heck is *Hamlet*?

ROSHI. IT'S BASICALLY A SHIT VERSION OF *THE LION
KING*.
THERE'S THIS BLOKE CALLED HAMLET
HAMLET IS LIKE THE ORIGINAL FUCKBOY
HE'S LIKE IF SIMBA WAS A BASIC BITCH
SO THERE ARE THESE TWO GUARDS
ONE OF THEM YOUS!!!!!
THEY'RE OUTSIDE FREEZIN THEIR BALLS OFF AND
THEY SEE A GHOST OF HAMLET'S DEAD DAD
AND THEY'RE LIKE OHMYGOD THAT'S SO
RANDOM
WE SHOULD TELL HAMLET.
MEANWHILE, HAMLET'S DAD JUST DIED AND HIS
MUM GOT REMARRIED TO HAMLET'S UNCLE
SUPER-QUICK.
HE'S GOT THAT FEELIN WHEN YOUS GO TO THE
MALL AND SEE CHRISTMAS DECORATIONS THE
DAY AFTER HALLOWEEN.
HAMLET'S MUM IS LIKE A HUMAN PROP WHO DOES
FUCK-ALL.
LIKE SHAKEY P JUST WHEELS HER OUT BUT SHE
DOESN'T REALLY DO ANYTHIN.
SHE'S A PERSONALITY VACUUM.
SO HAMLET'S DEAD DAD COMES UP TO HAMLET
AND IS LIKE
YO YOUR UNCLE IS A TWAT AND HE MURDERED ME
I WAS HAVIN A NAP AND HE'S ALL LIKE TAKE SOME
EAR POISON
HAMLET IS LIKE SHOCKED PIKACHU FACE.
HAMLET'S DEAD DAD IS LIKE LOL YEAH YOUS
SHOULD PROBABLY KILL HIM.
BUT I'M LIKE HMMM HOLD ON
WHY HAS THE GHOST WAITED NEARLY A MONTH
SINCE THE MARRIAGE BEFORE SHOWIN ITSELF?

BUT HAMLET'S DEAD DAD IS LIKE GOTTAGOBYE
AND THEN FOR LIKE MOST OF THE PLAY HAMLET
FUCKS AROUND AND PROCRASTINATES
HAMLET GETS DEPRESSED BECAUSE HE ISN'T AS
COOL AS SIMBA.
HAMLET'S EVIL UNCLE DOESN'T EVEN SING 'BE
PREPARED' SO HE CAN FUCK RIGHT OFF
HAMLET WAS SEEIN THIS GIRL OPHELIA
ANOTHER HUMAN PROP
HE'D SLIDE INTO HIS DM 'U UP BABE'
OPHELIA IS LIKE 'YEAHS' LIKE
HAMLET IS LIKE 'HERE'S A CAT PICTURE'
OPHELIA IS LIKE 'OHMYGOD I LOVE YOU'.
AND THEN HAMLET SETS OUT TO AVENGE HIS
FATHER'S MURDER
AND GETS HIS ENTIRE FAMILY AND EVERYONE
ELSE IN THE PLAY KILLED
SO BASICALLY HAMLET DECIDES TO PUT ON A SHIT
SHOW AND IS ALL LIKE
WITH JAZZ HANDS I WILL MAKE MY UNCLE
CONFESS TO MURDER
BUT IT DOESN'T WORK
AND HAMLET IS LIKE REALLY SURE IT NEARLY
WORKED CUZ HIS UNCLE FARTS OR SOMETHIN
THEN HE ACCIDENTALLY KILLS OPHELIA'S DAD
BECAUSE HE HATES THE CURTAINS IN THE ROOM.
AND THEN OPHELIA FALLS IN A PUDDLE AND
DROWNS AND EVERYONE'S LIKE WHATEVER
AND HAMLET GOES TO HER FUNERAL LIKE
FEEL LIKE SHIT JUST WANT HER BACK.
POUNDLAND TIMON AND PUMBAA DIE AND LIKE
NO ONE GIVES A FUCK
HAMLET GETS CASUALLY KIDNAPPED BY PIRATES
JUST CUZ...
AND THEN HAMLET'S MUM IS ALL LIKE
LOL I'M THIRSTY AND DRINKS SOME POISON
AND EVERYONE'S LIKE WHATEVER
AND HAMLET FINALLY KILLS HIS UNCLE.
AND HAMLET KILLS LAERTES.

AND LAERTES KILLS HAMLET.
AND ALL OF THIS COULD HAVE BEEN STOPPED
IF
AT
ANY
POINT
SOMEONE

ANYONE

TOLD HAMLET TO

SHUT

THE

FUCK UP!!!!!!!!

SONNY. sounds shit

ROSHI. IT'S OKAY I WAS ONCE A YOUNG
SHAKESPEAREAN ACTOR LIKE YOUS AND NOW
LOOK AT ME!
YOUS GONNA BE AMAZIN SONNY.

SONNY. B-B-B-BUSY!

ROSHI. YOU'LL NEVER SEE ME AGAIN AFTER I PLAY
HAMLET
CUZ I'LL SPEND ALL MY DAYS DOIN COKE WITH
JUDI DENCH.

SONNY. WHH-WHH-WHAT

THE

FUCK'S

A

JUDI

DENCH!!!!!?

9

School hall.
Lunchtime.

A terrified-looking SONNY *is standing next to* CAPTAIN
CHATTER *holding a* Hamlet *script.*

I feel like ROSHI *is now dressed like a theatre luvvie wearing a*
scarf and fancy sunglasses and looking FABULOUS AS FUCK.

FISH. Welcome to Lunch Time Drama Club.
I'll Lock The Doors. Just A Joke. I've Locked Them Already.

ROSHI. WELCOME EVERYONE TO THE RSC.
ROSHI'S SHAKESPEARE COMPANY.
THERE'S ANOTHER RSC WHO STOLE OUR NAME.
WE'RE IN A TURF WAR.
THEY SENT ME A BROCHURE.
I SENT THEM SOME POO.

FISH. Excuse Me –

ROSHI. THE OTHER RSC WILL PROBS DO A DRIVE-BY
SO YOUS ALL HAVE TO BE WILLIN TO SACRIFICE
YOURSELVES.

FISH. Excuse Me –

ROSHI. NO AUTOGRAPHS PLEASE.

FISH. Let's Begin.
I Have To Leave In Five Minutes
I Have A Meeting With My Cats But You All Carry On.
Remember You're Here To Have Fun. Jason Stop Smiling.
Okay From The Beginning.
My Guards, Take It Away!

VOICE OF GUARD. WHO GOES THERE!!!!!?

SONNY. !!!
!!

THE SKULL *in* ROSHI's *hand starts talking.*

THE SKULL. You're gonna dieeeeeeeeeeeeeeeeeeeeeeee!

SONNY. !!!!!!!!!!!!!!!!!!!!!!!!!!!!!!!!!!!!!!!
!!!
!!!
!!!

WILLIAM SHAKESPEARE *begins to climb out from the pages of the script.*

!!
!!
!!
!!

WILLIAM SHAKESPEARE *bites the head off another student.*

!!
!!
!!
!!
!!

CAPTAIN CHATTER *is scanning the script.*

CAPTAIN CHATTER. YOU WON'T BE ABLE TO SAY THIS WITHOUT STAMMERING!!
THE LETTER A, S AND U IN ONE SENTENCE!!
AND THEN A U AND ANOTHER S AND ANOTHER S AND ANOTHER S!!!
AHHHHHHHHHHHHHHHHHHHHHHHHHHHH!!!!!!!

CAPTAIN CHATTER *brings out a spade and bucket and starts digging like a madman.*

IF WE BOTH DIG WE'LL BE IN AUSTRALIA BY TEA TIME!!!!

SONNY. *Ahh-ahh-ahh-ahh–*

WILLIAM SHAKESPEARE *lunges for* CAPTAIN CHATTER. *They fight.*

WILLIAM SHAKESPEARE *punches* CAPTAIN CHATTER.

CAPTAIN CHATTER. USE THE POWER OF WORD AVOIDANCE!
SKIP THE WORD 'ANSWER', PRETEND YOU MISSED IT, MOVE STRAIGHT ONTO THE WORD 'STAND'. BOOM!

CAPTAIN CHATTER *punches* WILLIAM SHAKESPEARE.

SONNY. *Shh-shh-shh-shh-shh-shh-shh-shh-shh-shh-*STAND!

CAPTAIN CHATTER *uses his superpowers to push* WILLIAM SHAKESPEARE *back.*

SONNY *has an involuntary pause on the word 'and'.*

WILLIAM SHAKESPEARE *begins to strangle* CAPTAIN CHATTER.

WILLIAM SHAKESPEARE *brings out his giant quill.*

He spins it around and aims it at CAPTAIN CHATTER.

AH-AH-AH-AH-AH-AH-AHHHHHH!

WILLIAM SHAKESPEARE *uses his giant quill to stab* CAPTAIN CHATTER *who falls down dead.*
WILLIAM SHAKESPEARE *uses his quill like a MASSIVE MACHINE GUN to fire out letters at* SONNY.
As the letters touch him he screams an anguished cry full of pain and sorrow.
SONNY *is drowning in an ever growing sea of letters.*
He starts brutally slapping his face with two hands, trying anything to get the words out.

WAINWRIGHT *appears heroically soaring in the sky.*

WAINWRIGHT. TAKE MY HAND!

WAINWRIGHT *swoops down and lifts* SONNY, *saving him.*
SONNY *grabs* WAINWRIGHT's *hand tightly.*
They soar.

SAY THE WORDS SONNY! JUST SAY THE WORDS!!!!!!!!!

SONNY'S MUM *appears.*

SONNY *points. He tries to speak but gets stuck in an involuntary pause.*
SONNY'S MUM *looks through a pile of rotting letters sobbing and shaking, she's desperately trying to put them together to form words to express herself.*
SONNY *begs and pleads but* WAINWRIGHT *doesn't understand.*
SONNY'S MUM *begins sobbing louder, she's pulling her hair and slapping her face.*

SONNY'S MUM. DON'T COME IN! DON'T COME IN!

SONNY *lets go. He falls.*

FISH. ENOUGH!!!

Enough.

I Think We'll Just Move On.

We Only Have An Hour.

SONNY*'s soul rots.*

10

WAINWRIGHT*'s office.*
After school.

WAINWRIGHT. If you really want to make communicating easier for yourself, this requires your full attention –

SONNY. Miss! *I–I-I-*Is that – (*An involuntary pause on the letter 'a'.*)
a *L-L-*Lego *Mhh-Mhh-Mhh-Millennium Fa-Falcon*!?
SIIIIIIIIIIIIIIIICK.

WAINWRIGHT. Full attention.

SONNY *goes to touch it.*

NOOOOOOOO DON'T TOUCH IT!!

I mean, *whatever,* don't touch it.

You like *Star Wars* then!?

SONNY. Yeaa –

WAINWRIGHT. Favourite one?

SONNY. *A-a-a-Attack of the Clones.*

WAINWRIGHT. FUCK OFF!
  Sorry.

SONNY. *U-u-u-u*-used *t-t-t-*to *whh-whh-whh*-watch *i-i-i-*it *whh-m-my* with Mum.

WAINWRIGHT. What else did you do with your mum?

  SONNY'S MUM *suddenly and quickly walks through the scene.*

SONNY. *W-w-*we *g-g-g-*gonna *shh-shh-shh-shh*-start thh-then?

WAINWRIGHT. This is a *tough process* so your commitment must be total. *Okay?*

  SONNY *nods yes.*

  Okay!?

SONNY. *Y-*yes!

WAINWRIGHT. *OKAAAY!?*
  Stop avoiding words.
  Every time you substitute one word for another you're just making this harder.
  Okaaaaaaay?

  SONNY *dreads the vowel.*

SONNY. Ugh – *O-o-o-o-kay.*

WAINWRIGHT. I want you to *say* yes or no to the following questions. Okay?

  SONNY *nods.*

Sonny I want to hear your natural spontaneous brilliant way of speaking

SONNY. Ugh – *O-o-o-o-kay!*

WAINWRIGHT. When you think, do you stammer?

SONNY *shakes his head no.*

Please say.

SONNY. *N-n-n*-no.

WAINWRIGHT. When you sing do you stammer?

SONNY. Don't *s-s-s*-sing *M*-Miss!

WAINWRIGHT. Bullshit. You sing in the shower.
If you're speaking alone, do you stammer?

SONNY. *N-n-n-n-n*-never.

WAINWRIGHT. I bet, to you, those moments feel like magic don't they?

SONNY. *H-h-h*-how *y*-yous *knhh-knhh*-knows *M*-Miss?

WAINWRIGHT. I know everything, obviously.

SONNY. T-t-that why your *h-h*-head's *shh-shh-so* massive?

WAINWRIGHT. Let's just read through your scene from *Hamlet*.

SONNY. !!!!

WAINWRIGHT. Sonny relax. It's just a scene.

SONNY. I *ahh-ahh-ahh-ahh*-am *rhh-rhh-rhh*-relaxed!

WAINWRIGHT. He says while clenching his fist.
You literally look like you're straining for a shit.

SONNY. *M-M-M-M*-Miss, *I-I-I won't be able to shh-shh-shh-shh* saaaaaay this!

WAINWRIGHT. Let's just say your first two words which are 'Answer me.'

SONNY. UGHHHHHHHH!

WAINWRIGHT. Come on.
'WHO GOES THERE?'

THE LETTER A appears. SONNY looks terrified.

SONNY. !!!!!!!

THE LETTER A looks to SONNY ready to attack. Ready to kill.

WAINWRIGHT. The more you worry about stammering, the more tension you create.

An infestation of THE LETTER A fills the office. There's a fuck ton of them. CHAOS.

Don't worry about stammering.

SONNY. !!!!!!!!!!!

WAINWRIGHT. Sonny keep looking me in the eyes.

SONNY. !!!!!!!!!!!!!!

WAINWRIGHT. Who Goes There!?

SONNY. !!!!!!!!!!!!!!!

WAINWRIGHT. These Vowels Pop Up Everywhere And There's Nothing We Can Do About Them
But What We Can Do Is *Sliiiiiiide* Over Them.

SONNY opens his mouth, he can't bring himself to make any sound.

AAAAAAAAAAANSWER ME.

The infestation of THE LETTER A begins attacking SONNY.

Spend as long as you like elongating the initial sound.
Resist any feeling of <u>h</u>urry or pressure.

The infestation of THE LETTER A is holding him down.

Everyone else can wait.

SONNY. !!!!!!!!!!!!!!!!!!!!

WAINWRIGHT. Keep looking at me in the eyes.
    Don't look at the carpet, the carpet hasn't got eyes.
    What colour are my eyes Sonny?
    What colour are my eyes?

SONNY. P-P-P-P-PUDDLE G-G-G-G-GREY!!

WAINWRIGHT. SONNY MY EYES ARE BLUE!!!

SONNY. I-I-I-I-IT'S NOT MY FAULT YOUR BLUE *E-E-E-*
    E– YES LOOK PPPHH-PUDDLE GREY!!!

The infestation of THE LETTER A *begins attacking* SONNY
again.

SONNY *wails.*

WAINWRIGHT. SONNY SAY THE WORDS
    I PROMISE SONNY THAT WHATEVER H̲APPENS
    I WILL LISTEN.

*A quiet determination brews. It starts with a firmness which
grows into a forcefulness.*

THE LETTER A *will never quite be the same again.*

SONNY. *A-a-a–*
    Aaaaaaaaaaaaaaaaaaaaaaaaaaaaaaaaaaaaaaaaaaaaanswer me
    AAAAAAAAAAAAAAAAAAAAAAAAAAAAAAAAAAAAAA
    AAAAAANSWER ME
    A-A-AAAAAAAAA-ANSWER ME!!!!!!!

A look of wonder beams onto SONNY*'s face which
transforms into an enthusiastic smile.*

11

WAINWRIGHT*'s office.*
After school.

SONNY. *Ahh-ahh-ahh-ahh–*
Aaaaaaaaaaaaaaaaaaaaaaaaaaaaaaaaaaaaaaaaaaanswer me
SHH-SHHHHHHHHHH-SHHHHHHHHHHHHH-
SHHHHHHHHHHHHHH

WAINWRIGHT. You're trying to get the word out fluently.

SONNY. *SHH-SHH-SHH-SHH-SHH-SHH-SHH-SHH-SHH-*
SHH–

WAINWRIGHT. Why wrestle with that letter so <u>h</u>ard?
Slow it down and let the block complete itself and then slide.

SONNY *frustratedly throws the script on the floor.*

Pick it up.
Try talking relaxed like I told you.

SONNY. *Ahh-ahh-ahh-ahh–*
Aaaaaaaaaaaaaaaaaaaaaaaaaaaaaaaaaaaaaaaaaaanswer me
SHHHHHHHHHH!! SHHHHHHHHHHHHHH!!
SHHHHHHHHHHHHHH!!
Aaaaaaaaaaaaaaaaaaaand unnnnnfooold –

WAINWRIGHT. *Stand.* You skipped the word stand.

SONNY. UGH!!! *Ahh-ahh-ahh-ahh-*
Aaaaaaaaaaaaaaaaaaaaaaaaaaaaaaaaaaaaaaaaaaanswer me!

SHHHHHHHHHH!! SHHHHHHHHHHHHHH!!
SHHHHHHHHHHHHHH!!

SONNY *throws his script at* WAINWRIGHT.

*P-P-P-P-P-P-P-*PISS –
(*An involuntary pause on the word 'off'.*)
(*He gives up.*)

WAINWRIGHT. Finish it.

SONNY. I want you to finish it.

CAPTAIN CHATTER *crashes a lorry into the office.*

CAPTAIN CHATTER. *I DON'T LIKE THE WAY SHE'S
TALKING TO YOU ONE BIT!
LET'S TEACH HER A LESSON!*

SONNY. Y-y-y-y-y-you're –
(*An involuntary pause on the word 'a'.*)
*a LHH-LHH-LHH-*LOSER *M-M-M-M-*MISS!
*THH-THH-THH-*THE *O-O-O-*ONLY THH-THING *YUUH-
YUUH-YUUH-*YOU *DHH-*DO IS WATCH *S-S-S-STAR
WARS* AND *E-E-E-*EAT *RHH-*RYVITA!

WAINWRIGHT. That's *embarrassingly accurate.*

SONNY. I-I-I-IDIOT!

SONNY *picks up one of her posh pencils and snaps it.*

WAINRIGHT. Tell me h̲ow you're feeling?

SONNY. *Y-Y-Y-*YOU'RE *T-T-*TOO *SHH-SHH-SHH-*STUPID
TO TEACH ME S-S-S-S-STUFF.
*N-N-N-*NONE OF IT IS WORKIN!

WAINWRIGHT. You just need to give it time!

SONNY. *N-N-N-*NOT *WHH-W-W-W–*

CAPTAIN CHATTER. THE WORDS AREN'T COMING
OUT!

SONNY. *YOU'RE –* (*Trying to say shit.*) *S-S-S-S-S-S-S-*

CAPTAIN CHATTER. THE WORDS AREN'T COMING
OUT!

SONNY *picks up another posh pencil.*

SONNY. *S-S-S-S-S-S-S–* (*Grabs a glass from the desk.*)

CAPTAIN CHATTER. CONSTRICTION IN THROAT!!!!!

SONNY *lifts the glass.*

REVERT BACK TO PLAN A!
*LET'S SMASH THAT GLASS IN HER FUCKING FACE!
LET'S DESTROY THE WORLD AND WATCH IT BURN!*

WAINWRIGHT. IT WORKS FOR ME!!!!

SONNY....

WAINWRIGHT. I'm sorry Sonny, I didn't mean to…

H is my worst letter.

Growing up they all said it's only in your mind.

I read because you couldn't speak in a library.

I grew a deeper love of language and go to university
and one night
I meet an amazing woman who is kind and patient
and somehow manages to get my number and she rings me.
Of course, I don't answer.
I never speak on the phone.
She rings me again and again and again
I'm making her sound like a *stalker* but I promise you she
isn't

Suddenly she stops ringing…

Thank God I ran into her in Boots.

She's scared of ants.
She claps whenever a plane lands.

She pays attention to what I'm saying and not the way I'm
saying it.

Years later we decide to get married,
it's an excuse for me and Harry to get pissed with our mates.
That's her name, by the way, Harry.

Wedding planning.
Who knew there were so many types of flowers?
Vow writing.
Speaking in public.
The dreaded H.

No.

I will pronounce the woman's name I love perfectly.

I try some speech therapy

Wedding Day.

Ahh.

We walk down the aisle to Joni Mitchell.
and you <u>h</u>ave no idea who the fuck Joni Mitchell is do you?

Vow time.
I take thee Hhh–

SONNY. !!!

WAINWRIGHT. And I stammer my Fucking <u>H</u>ead Off.

SONNY. WHAT!! MISSSSSS!

WAINWRIGHT. And I Was Glorious.

SONNY....

WAINWRIGHT. Look, overcoming stammering doesn't mean
not stammering
Overcoming stammering means overcoming the idea that
stammering can hold you back.

SONNY....

WAINWRIGHT. I still have scary days when I feel the very
struggle of dragging up every single H
But I now have no fear of the monsters who once ate up all
my words.

So no, Sonny,
I guess you think I <u>h</u>ave no idea what you're going through.
Because I'm old as fuck and have a massive vagina.
But I do know you draw so well because you find talking
difficult
and your brilliant mind is a thesaurus switching out word
after word after word.

I have spoken to fluent people and a lot of them are
VeryFuckingBoring.
I have spoken to people who stammer
I have seen them <u>h</u>old entire rooms in the palm of their
<u>h</u>ands.

Until you accept that you stammer you will be powerless

you may think you're not,
because you can throw things,
Or you manage a whole day without speaking

but make no mistake

you <u>h</u>ave no real power...
Now may I <u>h</u>ave my glass back please?

SONNY *hands the glass back.*

WAINWRIGHT. I can give you another <u>h</u>our?

SONNY *nods yes.*

Speak.

I can <u>g</u>ive you another <u>h</u>our?

Please speak.

SONNY. O-o-o-o-okay.

WAINWRIGHT. Who goes there?

12

WAINWRIGHT*'s office.*
Mid-morning.

She sits marking.
FISH *enters carrying a tin of Roses.*

FISH. Open Sesame! Just A Joke, I Opened The Door With My
    Hands.

WAINWRIGHT. Can't speak.

FISH. Have A Chocolate?

WAINWRIGHT. I'm fine.

FISH. Have A Chocolate. It's Paul's Last Day.

WAINWRIGHT. Why are we celebrating another amazing teacher resigning?

FISH. Take One.

WAINWRIGHT. I said I'm fine.

FISH. And I Said *Take One*. I Would Have One Myself But I Don't Eat Solids So I Can Spend More Time Licking My Cats.
Now Take One.

WAINWRIGHT. Fine. Do I pick between the processed fat or the processed fat?

FISH. Glad I Ran Into You Actually –

WAINWRIGHT. Barged in screaming with chocolates –

FISH. Now you know I don't like you to see me as a boss –

WAINWRIGHT. Now you know I don't –

FISH. I haven't received any behaviour reports from you in weeks?

WAINWRIGHT. Are we still doing them?

FISH. Yes we are *'still doing them'*.
They are extremely important to the rebranding of our school.
I met you halfway.
I wanted suspensions
you wanted lunchtime drama club.
None of those kids are natural actors.
They run around like maniacs!

WAINWRIGHT. Don't you wish we could just euthanise them? It would make running this school so much easier.

FISH *is BIG into this idea, probably daydreaming about the spreadsheet already.*

It was a joke.

FISH. You had sessions earlier.
    What were you doing?

WAINWRIGHT. Listening to the students.

FISH. Stop That.
    I Need Some *Real Evidence Of Improvement* In The
    Students.
    Now Take A Chocolate You.
    Not That You Deserve One Naughty.

    WAINWRIGHT*'s hand hovers around the tin.*

WAINWRIGHT. I'm fine thank you.
    Is there anything else I can help you with?
    It's just I've got Roshi –

FISH. Did You Not Get The Email?

WAINWRIGHT. You're just across the hall from me, we don't
    need to email.
    You could just whisper, the walls are thin enough.

FISH. I've Expelled Her.
    (*She notices the Lego* Millennium Falcon.)
    This Is Silly.

    WAINWRIGHT *is struck by the news.*

WAINWRIGHT. You didn't have to do that.
    She was getting better.
    She was excited about the play.

FISH. She Strangled Chantelle Green.
    (*She fiddles with the Lego Millennium Falcon.*)
    How Silly!

WAINWRIGHT. You could have spoken to her, you could have –

FISH. Frankly Her Grades Weren't Great As Well.
    I *Couldn't* Have *Spoken* To Her.
    No One Can Speak To Her.

WAINWRIGHT. You could have tried!

    I'm sorry.

Young people aren't like your Cats, they don't meow when
they need something –

FISH. Oh No, My Cats Never Meow.

WAINWRIGHT. These kids here
they're like those dodgy cheap fireworks which explode too
quickly.
These lot, these *brilliant mad* lot, they're born in the cracks
and they're just trying to crawl their way out and express
themselves in any way possible
and you just push them back in
no not push,
throw.

Due to FISH's fiddling, the Lego collapses.

FISH. Ooops.

She picks up a piece of Lego and holds it in her hand.

Stop Whatever This Is And Start Doing *My* Behaviour
Development Scheme.
Now Take A Chocolate.

FISH *holds out the tin.*

WAINWRIGHT*'s hand hovers.*

She takes a chocolate.

And Swallow.

She does.

WAINWRIGHT *holds out her hand for the Lego piece.*
FISH *coldly drops it on the floor and exits.*

WAINWRIGHT *begins to rebuild the Lego, piece by piece.*
She rebuilds a small amount.
Suddenly she trashes the rebuilt pieces with a rageful fury.

FUCK!

Tears begin to stream down her eyes as she stands
surrounded by scattered Lego pieces.

13

School hall.
Lunchtime.

SONNY *is standing amongst students who are playing with*
words.

CAPTAIN CHATTER *is using* SONNY*'s vocal cords as a jump*
rope or some mad shit like that.

SONNY *grabs back his vocal cords and inserts them back in.*
After some trepidation, he joins in with the other students.
At first he's nervous.
But later he's laughing, electrified and passionate.
He speaks.
He speaks.
He speaks.
For the first time in SONNY*'s life, language looks like a game*
and not a battle.

A forest grows from his mouth.

ROSHI *watches onwards looking sad and lonely.*
An unstoppable rage grows inside of her.

14

The lockers.
After school.

ROSHI *is about to hide in a locker.*

Instead SONNY *jumps out one MAKING* ROSHI *SHIT*
HERSELF.

SONNY. Y-Y-YOUS S-SHAT AND PISSED YOURSELF A-
    AT THE S-SAME TIME!!!!

ROSHI. I WAS USIN MY AMAZING ACTIN SKILLS CUZ
    I FELT SORRY FOR YOUS

SONNY. What *y*-yous doin here?

ROSHI. CAN'T MISS YOUR BIRTHDAY.
    STOLE YOUS A GERBIL FROM PETS AT HOME.
    CATCH!

    ROSHI *throws a gerbil at* SONNY.

    THE SECURITY GUARD KEPT FOLLOWIN ME
    AROUND
    AT FIRST I THOUGHT IT'S CUZ I TRIED TO STEAL
    THAT PUFFERFISH LAST WEEK.
    BUT IT'S CUZ I'M FAMOUS NOW BECAUSE I
    PLAYED HAMLET.
    I WAS LIKE DON'T TOUCH ME PEASANT.
    I GAVE EVERYTHING I HAVE TO MY PUBLIC ON
    THAT STAGE
    I AM ENTITLED TO SOME PRIVACY AND SOME FREE
    GERBILS.
    (*She grabs* SONNY'*s dictionary.*) SHITTTT! WHYS YOUS
    READIN THIS THESAURUS?

SONNY. Mrs Wainwright gave me –
    N-n-no *re-re-reason*!

ROSHI. WHYS YOUS READIN THIS!?
    I NEVER SEES YOUS THESE DAYS!

SONNY. I *s*-sent yous v-voicenotes!

ROSHI. I NEVER SEES YOUS THESE DAYS!

SONNY. Yous bein *ppppp*Preposterous.

    SONNY *smiles that he had the confidence to say the word.*

ROSHI. I can't believe yous thirteen!
    Can yous believe yous thirteen!?
    Whats time was yous born?

SONNY....

ROSHI. Shit, don't yous know?
   Didn't she ever tells yous?
   Does yous even remember *anythin* bout her?

SONNY. We u-u-u-u-*uuu*used t-t-to climb to the top of this hill.
   *SSSSS*O SSSO SSSO high.
   Shhh-she *was aaaalways sssss*scared but I weren't.
   From way up all the people didn't look like ants, just tiny
   people.
   Was – (*An involuntary pause.*) amazin.
   N-nothin u-used to scare me until…

   Ssssshe started to hate noise
   And then ssssshe sssstarted to hate light
   And then ssssshe started to hate me.

ROSHI. Yous should chat about her more Sonny.

   How's lunchtime drama club goin?

SONNY. Quit aaaaaages aaaaago.

   ROSHI *punches* SONNY *on the arm.*

   Owwwwwww!

ROSHI. You're a motherfluffin liar Sonny.
   Last time when yous was havin a piss
   which yous said was a piss but it was blatantly a shit because
   yous took like ten minutes.
   I had a look in your bag and saw your script notes!

   I miss it.
   That's stupid ain't it?
   But I miss it.
   I miss havin somethin that was mine.
   Even if I wasn't amazin at it

   at least

   It Was Mine.

   So do yous miss me?

SONNY. Yous bein *m-m*-Monotonous.

SONNY *smiles and does a little excitable fist pump.*

YOUS BEIN UUUUUNSTIMULATIN.

ROSHI. Say yous miss me!

SONNY. Naaaah!

ROSHI. Say yous miss me!

ROSHI *jumps on top of him.*

SAAAAY IT!

SONNY. Can't say it, got a stammer!

ROSHI. SAAAAY IT!

SONNY. OKAY, OKAY, MISS YOUS!

NOTTTTTTTTTT!!

I'm *s*-sorry! I'm *s*-sorry!

NOTTTTTTTTTT!!

ROSHI. WHEN I COME WATCH *HAMLET* I'M THROWIN TOMATOES.

SONNY. *L-l-l*-like Miss Fish will let yous *i*-in after you s-s-sstrangled Chantelle –

ROSHI *instantly stops play fighting. She's still and silent.*

ROSHI. She said that?

SONNY. Y-yeah…

ROSHI. oh.

i go in there, just to chat.
chantelle freaks out and calls mrs pearl and she starts cryin and sayin shit.
no one even asks me what happened.
it's like they already decided.
they already decided what i did
who i am.
decided even before i have.

yous wait
i'm goin in tomorrow at lunch to see her
just yous wait!

SONNY. *N-n-n–*

ROSHI. YOUS JUST WAIT!

SONNY. LLLLLLISTEN –

ROSHI....

SONNY. Yous go back in there, you'll just make it worse.

SONNY *goes back to reading the thesaurus.*

ROSHI. Not-Alan says they're lookin for a new Captain
Birdseye
so maybe I'll apply for that instead.

SONNY. *H-*his name's M-Michael by the way.

ROSHI. HOW YOUS KNOW?

SONNY. A-a-asked.

ROSHI. !!!!!!!!!!!!!!!!!

SONNY....

ROSHI. Do yous like your gerbil?

SONNY. Yea.

ROSHI. I can fit a whole gerbilin my mouth?
Wanna see?

SONNY. Nah.

ROSHI. WANNA GO SMOKE CIGARETTE BUTTS OFF
THE FLOOR?

SONNY. Not sssssssssssssssmoooked for aaaaaaages. Mrs
Wainwright sssssays it's bad for yous.

ROSHI. Oh.
We hangin tomorrow yeah?

SONNY. Can't. Drama club rehearsal.

ROSHI. Oh. Next week then?

SONNY....

ROSHI. Sonny, when yous was told I strangled Chantelle did
    yous believe them?

SONNY....

ROSHI. Thought so.

15

WAINWRIGHT*'s office.*
After school.

SONNY *runs in. He's extremely hyper.*
The office has been packed into boxes but SONNY *doesn't*
notice.

SONNY. MISS! MISSSSSS!
    I DID IT!!!!
    GUESS WHAT I O-ORDERED FOR LUNCH FROM THE
    CANTEEN?
    G-GUESS WHAT I O-ORDERED!!!!!!!!!?

WAINWRIGHT....ecstasy?

SONNY. *A-A*ND I WAS LIKE TO THE DINNER LADY M-
    MONDAYS AM I RIGHT?
    A-AND SHE WAS LIKE MONDAYS AM I RIGHT?
    AND IT WAS A REALLY BORIN CONVERSATION BUT
    I DID IT!!!
    A-AND THEN I ORDERED E-EVERYTHIN FROM THE
    CANTEEN AND
    w-w-what...

Silence.
SONNY*'s world breaks.*

WAINWRIGHT *keeps packing.*
Her world is probably breaking as well.
She keeps packing.

WAINWRIGHT. Finish your sentence.

SONNY. W-w-w-w-w-ww-what yous *dhh*-doin?

WAINWRIGHT. I'm sorry.

SONNY. *S-S-S-S*TOP!
*Sssssssss*stop.
Ssssssssstop. Y-y-y-yous can't!

WAINWRIGHT. I'm sorry people keep leaving you and I'm
   sorry I've become one of them.

SONNY. NO!
   Yous bein *DDDDISCOURTEOUS*!
   Yous bein III*INCONSIDERATE*!
   Yous bein *IIIIILL-MANNERED*!

WAINWRIGHT. Somebody's been reading that thesaurus
   I gave them.

SONNY. YOUS BEIN A CUNT!

WAINWRIGHT....

SONNY. *W-w-w-w*-what about me!?
    Yous just *g-g-g*-goin!?
   W-w-w-what about me!? –

WAINWRIGHT. WHAT ABOUT ME!?
   Sorry.
   Because it's always about you and it's never about us.
   I'm tired, Sonny.

She sits down looking broken and in pain.

SONNY....

WAINWRIGHT....

   SONNY *is about to walk out.*

SONNY'S MUM *appears and makes it clear to him if he walks out now he will regret it for the rest of his life.*

SONNY *folds up paper into a paper plane and flies it to* WAINWRIGHT.

SONNY. Miss, *y-y-*your sorry face looks like a *c-*constipated face.

WAINWRIGHT. Your paper plane is shit.

A moment.

Who goes there?

SONNY *stands by the exit unsure whether to respond.*

Who goes there?
Oi, don't be a dickhead.

SONNY. *Ah-ah-ah-ah-ah-ah answer me*
ssss… stand,
and *u-u-u-u-u-u–*

I had it this lunch Miss!

WAINWRIGHT. Remember what I said about pushing.

SONNY. A-A-A-A-A-A-A-A-A–

WAINWRIGHT. K-k-keep your stammering soft and r-r-relaxed and you can ssssslide iiiiiinto the wwwords.

SONNY. A-A-A-A-A-A-A-A-A–

WAINWRIGHT. Doesn't it get exhausting?

SONNY. SHH-SHH-SHH–

WAINWRIGHT. Being so <u>H</u>ELL-BENT –

SONNY. SHH-SHH-SHH-SHH!!

WAINWRIGHT. Being so <u>H</u>OTHEADED –

SONNY. SHH-SHH-SHH-SHH AHHHHH!

WAINWRIGHT. Being kept <u>H</u>OSTAGE –

SONNY. SHH-SHH-SHH –

WAINWRIGHT. Judging your speech on <u>how</u> much you're stammering and not on what you're saying –

SONNY. SHH-SHH-SHH –

WAINWRIGHT. Tell me about *Star Wars*, you'd watch it with your mum right?

SONNY. U*h-uh-uh-uh-uh-uh* –

WAINWRIGHT. No. *Tell me* about your mum.

SONNY. *I-i-i-i-i-i*-it *w-w-w*-was… *F-F-FUCK Y-Y-Y-YOU M-M-M-MISS!*

WAINWRIGHT. Tell me.

SONNY. *C-c-c-c*-can't! –

WAINWRIGHT. How was it?

SONNY. *C-C-C-C*-CAN'T!

WAINWRIGHT. It must have been boring.

SONNY. *N-N-N–*

WAINWRIGHT. BORING!

SONNY. IT WAS AMAZIN! IT'S LIKE NOTHIN ELSE MATTERED! OUTSIDE THEM STREETS WERE BURNIN BUT INSIDE WE WAS FINE! BETTER THAN FINE, WE WAS *PERFECT*! WE WAS *PERFECT*!

WAINWRIGHT. How are you feeling right now?

SONNY. I FEEL I FEEL. I FEEL.

CAPTAIN CHATTER.…

SONNY. I'm sick of always feelin

CAPTAIN CHATTER.…

SONNY. ALWAYS FEELIN ALWAYS FEELIN ALWAYS FEELIN

CAPTAIN CHATTER.…

SONNY. Ashamed.

CAPTAIN CHATTER....

SONNY. I don't wanna feel *ah-ah-Ashamed*.
I just don't wanna feel *Ashamed*.
I wanna say hello!
I wanna say the answers in class!
I wanna soar!

I wanna tell people about my mum.
I wanna speak about her.

I want people to listen.

I wanna speak.

WAINWRIGHT. I know.

SONNY. I wanna speak.

WAINWRIGHT. I know.

SONNY. Would they wanna listen?

Cuz I think maybe they would?

WAINWRIGHT. Then Speak.

SONNY. when she started to get ill she'd sit on the edge of her bed for days

you don't need to talk to me
just let me see you
keep the door open

mum i can't walk home from here i don't know the way
i'm not too old for hugs

don't turn on the light
don't let the mash touch the beans
don't step on the creaky step

I'm sorry Mum

And then she made her first attempt

you don't need to love me

just stay

please just stay

I won't speak I won't speak I won't speak

Just stay

How dare the world continue after this.

WAINWRIGHT. Keep speaking about her Sonny. Keep. Speaking.

SONNY. If I had said something –

WAINWRIGHT. You Are Not To Blame –

SONNY. My mouth –

WAINWRIGHT. You Are Not To Blame –

SONNY. Last thing we spoke about was *fuckin Star Wars*! –

WAINWRIGHT. She wanted to speak about something you *love* and if you can't see that than you're an idiot.

SONNY....

WAINWRIGHT....

SONNY. You're an idiot.

She gave up on words but I don't wanna give up on words.

WAINWRIGHT. I know.

SONNY. I don't wanna give up on words Miss!

WAINWRIGHT. I know. I know.

SONNY. I don't wanna give up on words! I don't wanna give up on words!

WAINWRIGHT. It's okay.

SONNY. I don't wanna give up on words! I don't wanna give up on words!

I don't wanna give up on words!

CAPTAIN CHATTER *slowly waves goodbye*.

SONNY *waves goodbye back*. CAPTAIN CHATTER *disappears*.

Who goes there?
That's your line yea?

WAINWRIGHT. We don't need to do that right now.

SONNY. I wanna do it.
Who goes there?

WAINWRIGHT. It's fine.

SONNY. Miss I wanna do it!
WHO GOES THERE?

WAINWRIGHT. Who Goes There?

SONNY. *Ah-ah-ah-ah-answer me*
sssssstand,
and *u-u-u-u-u-u* uunfold yourselfff –

WAINWRIGHT. LONG LIVE THE KING! –

SONNY. *Bhhh-bhhh-bhhh-bhhh-bhhh*!!!!!! –

WAINWRIGHT. Bounce along with it smoooooooothly –

SONNY. bbbbbbBernardo –

WAINWRIGHT. Take as long as you want
Bernardo can wait.
He doesn't have a life –

SONNY. bbbbbbBernardo –

WAINWRIGHT. HE! –

SONNY. You *c-c-c-c-c-COMEE!*
most caaaarefully… *upon your… hour* –

WAINWRIGHT. *'TIS NOW STRUCK TWELVE; GET THEE TO BED, FRANCISCO*. –

SONNY (*speaking fast*).
FffffForThisReliefMuchThanksTisBitterColdAndIAm
SickAtHeart –

WAINWRIGHT. Don't rush through the sentence.
Enjoy it.
Let him have his little moan.
'Tis bitter cold, And I am sick at heart.
WHOOOOOO GOES THERE!? –

SONNY. A-a-a-a-UGHHH!

WAINWRIGHT. Every time your mind tries to make you feel
bad about stammering I want you to tell it to fuck off.
You are doing nothing wrong.
LET ME HEAR YOUR BRILLIANT VOICE SONNY
WHO GOES THERE!? –

SONNY. A-A-A-A-A-A-FUCK OFF! A-A-A-ANSWER
ME!! –

WAINWRIGHT. Brilliant –

SONNY. S-s-s-s-s-FUCK OFF! s-s-STAND!
A-a-a-a-FUCK OFF FUCK OFF FUCK OFF and
Uuuh-uuuh-FUCK OFF!!!! UNFOOOOOLD Y-Y-YOUR
SHH-SHH– FUCK OFF!! SELF!!! –

WAINWRIGHT. LONG LIVE THE KING!!! –

SONNY. bbbbbbbernardo –

WAINWRIGHT. HE! –

SONNY. You *c-c-c-c-c -COMEE!* most caaaaaarefully
u-u-u-u-u-u-u-u-u-upon
y-y-y-your… hour –

WAINWRIGHT. 'TIS NOW STRUCK TWELVE; GET THEE
TO BED, FRANCISCO –

SONNY. F-f-for this relief much thanks i-i-i-i-i-it is bitter cold
ahh-and I am shh-shh-shh-shh-shh-shh-shh-sick at heart –

WAINWRIGHT. You sound more indifferent at heart –

SONNY. S-SICK AT HEART!!!!!!!!!!

S-S-SICK AT HEART!!!!!!!!!!!!!!!!!! –

WAINWRIGHT. HAVE YOU HAD QUIET GUARD?
Don't be nervous about the S.

SONNY. Not a mouse sssssSTIRRING!!!!!!!! –

WAINWRIGHT. AND AGAIN WHO GOES THERE! –

*WILLIAM SHAKESPEARE ENTERS THE OFFICE WITH
A FUCKING CHAINSAW!!!!!!!!!!!!!!!!!!!!!!!!!!!!!!!!!*

SONNY *and* WAINWRIGHT *don't give a fuck.*

SONNY. *-A-A-A-A-ANSWER ME!!!!!!!!!*

SSSSSSSTAND!!!!!!!!!!!!

ANNNNNNND

UUUUUUNFOLDDDD YOURSELF!!!!!!!! –

Not a single fuck is given.

WAINWRIGHT. LONG LIVE THE KING!!! –

SONNY. *BBBBBBBBBBBERNARDO –*

WAINWRIGHT. HE!!

SONNY. *YOU COME MOST CAREFULLY UUUUUHPON
YOUR oooooHOUR!!!!! –*

*They start ballroom dancing or waltzing or something like
that with* WILLIAM SHAKESPEARE.

WAINWRIGHT. 'TIS NOW STRUCK TWELVE; GET THEE
TO BED, FRANCISCO –

WILLIAM SHAKESPEARE *is actually a big fan of this
dancing.*

SONNY. F-F-FOR THIS RELIEF MUCH THANKS IT IIS
BITTER COLD AND I AM SSSSICK AT HEART!!!!!!!!!! –

How delightful, thinks WILLIAM SHAKESPEARE.

WAINWRIGHT. HAVE YOU HAD QUIET GUARD? –

WILLIAM SHAKESPEARE *is loving life.*

SONNY. NO I S-S-STAMMERED MY F-FUCKING HEAD OFF!!! –

This is the most fun I've had in decades, thinks WILLIAM SHAKESPEARE.

WAINWRIGHT. AND AGAIN WHO GOES THERE? –

I stan Sonny, thinks WILLIAM SHAKESPEARE.

SONNY. *AAAAAAAANSWER ME!!!!!!!!!*

SSSSTAND!!!!!!!!!!!!

ANNNNNNND

UHH-UNFOLDDDD YOURSELF!!!!!!!! –

I must get him to sign my playtext, thinks WILLIAM SHAKESPEARE

WAINWRIGHT. WHO GOES THERE? –

The boy speaks rather beautifully, thinks WILLIAM SHAKESPEARE.

SONNY. *AAAAAANSWER ME!!!!!!!!!*

SSSSSSTAND!!!!!!!!!!!!

ANNNNNNND

UUUUUNFOLDDDD YOURSELF!!!!!!!!

WAINWRIGHT. WHO GOES THERE? –

SONNY (*sometimes fluent, sometimes stammering but always still speaking*). *ANSWER ME!!!!!!!!! STAND!!!!!!!!!!!! AND UNFOLD YOURSELF!!!!! ANSWER ME!!!!!!!!! STAND!!!!!!!!!!!! AND UNFOLD YOURSELF!!!!! ANSWER ME!!!!!!!!! STAND!!!!!!!!!!!! AND UNFOLD YOURSELF!!!!! ANSWER ME!!!!!!!!! STAND!!!!!!!!!!!! AND UNFOLD YOURSELF!!!!! ANSWER ME!!!!!!!!! STAND!!!!!!!!!!!! AND UNFOLD YOURSELF!!!!! ANSWER ME!!!!!!!!! STAND!!!!!!!!!!!! AND UNFOLD YOURSELF!!!!! ANSWER ME!!!!!!!!! STAND!!!!!!!!!!!! AND UNFOLD YOURSELF!!!!! ANSWER ME!!!!!!!!! STAND!!!!!!!!!!!! AND UNFOLD YOURSELF!!!!! ANSWER ME!!!!!!!!!*

STAND!!!!!!!!!!!!! AND UNFOLD YOURSELF!!!!! ANSWER ME!!!!!!!!! STAND!!!!!!!!!!!!! AND UNFOLD YOURSELF!!!!!

FISH *enters*.

FISH. Give Me And Mrs Wainwright Five Minutes.

FISH pours herself a coffee.
WAINWRIGHT looks like she's screaming internally.

Give Me And Mrs Wainwright Five Minutes.

SONNY exits.
But from offstage we hear him say to a rando.

SONNY. HI I'M ssssSONNY!!!!!!!!!!!!

WAINWRIGHT. I could listen to him speak all day.

FISH. I'd Much Prefer To Listen To White Noise.

WAINWRIGHT. You love coffee, don't you?
Why don't you just inject it and be done with?

FISH. Are These *My* Behaviour Development Forms?

FISH goes to grab them.
WAINWRIGHT quickly eats all the forms like some mad woman.

And then:

WAINWRIGHT. Passive-aggressive forms taste very bland.

FISH picks up the sugar.

You can't have that. That's *mine*.

FISH. Oh No
I *Never* Use Sugar.

She takes out her own sweetener from her pocket and pours it in.
Why the hell is this lady carrying her own sweetener around with her?

You, My Dear, Are Going To End Up With Diabetes If You Eat All That Sugar.
They'll Have To Cut Your Legs Off.
Pity. *Snip. Snip.*

WAINWRIGHT. You, my dear, are going to end up *shitting for days* because sweetener has a fuck ton of laxative in.
Pity. *Shit. Shit.*

No but seriously why is this lady carrying her own sweetener around with her? Who does that?

FISH. It's A Shame This Couldn't Work Out.

WAINWRIGHT. It's a shame I actually like young people.

FISH. It's A Shame You Couldn't Reach My Standards.

WAINWRIGHT. It's a shame you're a fucking psychopath!

FISH. Do You Have Any Behaviour Development Forms So I Can Give Them To Jane For The Handover.
I Want It All Streamlined Perfectly.

WAINWRIGHT. I h̲ave one left.
Ah! Ah! H̲old on!
I'll make a deal, I'll give them to you if you can name ten children in this school and what they *love*? –

FISH. No More Deals –

WAINWRIGHT. Okay too hard for you.
One child? –

FISH. Behaviour Development Reports? –

WAINWRIGHT. ONEE CHILD! COME ON! YOU CAN DO IT!

Slightly relieved you couldn't because I haven't done any in weeks –

FISH. What?

WAINWRIGHT. Not A Single One.
One child?
Jason Green
wanted to be a drummer, he couldn't afford a drum kit
no kid can around here and our music department is a puddle of wank
so he played the drums on everything he could

on tables
on walls
and even on <u>h</u>is fellow students' heads.
<u>H</u>is neighbour gave him a pound a week for cleaning her
'skanky' flat (<u>h</u>is words, not mine),
and <u>h</u>e's just got a second-hand drum kit
<u>h</u>e showed me a video of <u>h</u>im drumming on <u>h</u>is phone earlier
today
and <u>h</u>e's brilliant,
<u>h</u>e's bloody brilliant!
You should <u>h</u>ear him!

FISH. My Cats Don't Enjoy Drums And I Only Enjoy Lift
Music.
Is This What You've Been Doing During These Sessions?

WAINWRIGHT. Is this what you wanted to be when you were
younger?

FISH. Stop Being Naive!
The Whole Inspirational Teacher And Ooooh I Eat
Paperwork Thing Is Very Lovely
Very Fucking Lovely
But I'm On The Frontline Like Nicolas Cage Trying To Push
Us Up The League Tables!
Preparing The Evidence!
Showing The Inspectors Improvements!

AND ON TOP OF THIS MY CATS ARE EATING ME
ALIVE!!!!

I'M FORTY PER CENT FLESH IF THAT!!!!

THIS ARM IS JUST A STUMP!!!!!!!!!!!

If This Doesn't Work There Will Be No Leaving Parties
No Celebrations,
No Retirement Cards!
There Will Just Be *Failure*!
I Want Us To *Win*!
I Want *That Boy* Outside To *Win*! –

WAINWRIGHT. That boy <u>has</u> created beauty which you couldn't even comprehend because it <u>has</u> *nothing* to do with your stupid league tables or your fucking Cats!

FISH *brings out a baby monitor.*

FISH (*into the baby monitor*). Don't Listen To The Mean Lady! Mummy *Loves You*!

WAINWRIGHT....

FISH....

WAINWRIGHT. Are your Cats on the other end?

FISH. No. Maybe. Yes.

WAINWRIGHT. Give it to me.

FISH. No!

WAINWRIGHT. Give it to me!

WAINWRIGHT *snatches the baby monitor from Fish's hand.*

What's *Fuck You* in Cat?

FISH. Don't You Dare!

WAINWRIGHT (*into baby monitor*). *FUCK YOU CATS!!!!*

FISH *destroys the Lego* Millennium Falcon.

FISH. *AHHHHHHH HHHHHHHH!!!*

WAINWRIGHT. *FUCK YOU CATS!!!!!!!!*

FISH *starts eating the Lego* Millennium Falcon.

Both have gone fucking mental.

FISH. *LOOK I CAN EAT THINGS TOO!*

I CAN EAT THINGS TOO!

NOM! NOM! NOM!

The adults have become the children.
Anarchy.
SONNY *suddenly re-enters.*

They suddenly stop.

SONNY. Miss I need to go.

WAINWRIGHT....

FISH....

Good Meeting.

WAINWRIGHT. Good Meeting.

Before FISH *exits she coughs out some Lego and leaves it on the desk.*
She exits.

SONNY. WHOAAAAAAAAAAAAAAAAA!!!!!!!!! MISS WHAT WAS YOUS CHATTIN ABOUT?

WAINWRIGHT. The weather.

SONNY. Y-Y-YOUS WENT MENTAL MISS!!!!! DO IT a-a-AGAIN!!!! DO IT a-a-AGAIN!!!!.
S-S-S-Shit I need to go.
Got plans.

WAINWRIGHT. Look at you. Plans.

SONNY. G-g-goin out with Jackie.
You know she works o-o-o-one day a week as an assassin?
Money and taxes and stuff.

WAINWRIGHT. Acountant...

SONNY. *M-M-M-M-Miss* I just wanna say.
For what yous done.
I wanna say.

Suddenly SONNY *hugs* WAINWRIGHT *tighter than anyone has hugged anyone ever before.*

After a few moments of indecisiveness WAINWRIGHT *hugs him back.*

WAINWRIGHT. Crushing my lungs…

  Goodbye Sonny.

  Hey Sonny wait.

SONNY. What?

WAINWRIGHT.…

SONNY.…

WAINWRIGHT. You've got a shit handshake.

16

Backstage.
Ten minutes before the lunchtime performance of Hamlet.

SONNY *looks petrified.*
FISH *enters.*

FISH. Why Haven't You Got Your Costume On Yet!?
  I've Asked An Inspector To Watch The Show!
  Have You Seen Roshi On School Grounds Today?

SONNY. *N-n-n-no.*

FISH. You Would Say If You've Seen Roshi Yes?
  It's Very Serious.

SONNY. *AAAAAin't* seen her Miss.

FISH. Okay.

SONNY. If You Ever Need To Talk, My Door Is Always Open.
  Jason, Not Now I'm Busy.
  Jason I Don't Care If You're On Fire.
  Jason Everyone Here Is Clinically Dead. You're Not Special.

  FISH *exits.*

  S-s-she's gone.
  Why s s-s-he wanna s-see yous?

ROSHI *reveals herself from her hiding space.*
She seems more frantic than ever.

ROSHI. YOUS FIND THIS FUNNY.
NOT-ALAN CAME ROUND MINE FOR BREAKFAST,
DOESN'T EVEN BRING HIS OWN.
STINGY BITCH!

I POUR NOT-ALAN A BOWL OF CRUNCHY NUT
NOT-ALAN SAYS 'WAIT ROSHI HASN'T CRUNCHY
NUT GOT NUTS IN BECAUSE I'M ALLERGIC TO
NUTS?'
I SAY 'COURSE NOT, CRUNCHY NUTS AREN'T EVEN
CRUNCHY, THEY ALWAYS GO SOGGY.'

SONNY. W-w-whats yous d-d-done!? –

ROSHI. SO WE EAT,
EATIN AWAY,
MUNCH MUNCH MUNCH
MAKIN MUNCHY MEMORIES –
MUNCHIN MAKIN MEMORIES –

SONNY. Roshi! –

ROSHI. TURNS OUT THEY HAVE GOT NUTS IN AND
NOT-ALAN'S FACE GETS MASSIVE –

SONNY. WHATS YOUS DONE!?

ROSHI....

ROSHI *slowly unzips her hoodie. Her top is covered in*
blood.

SONNY. !!!

ROSHI. I came to school to look for *yous* but *yous* weren't
there!
So I go and find Chantelle Green.
She's in the park.
I just wanna know why she said what she said, that's all.
The words are in my head.
'Why yous say it Chantelle?'

'Why yous say it Chantelle?'
'Why yous say it Chantelle?'
She starts sayin stuff,
real nasty stuff from her nasty mouth.
And there's a brick and I…

Called the ambulance straight away
bolted it when they came.
Whilst I'm waitin,
I'm holdin me hands

against her

against her

tryin to stop the

there's so much.

I'm what they said I was

I'm thinkin
I'm thinkin bout DT class.
We had to make these wooden boxes

everyone else's was propa brilliant

and mine was wonky and crooked.

Why couldn't my box be like theirs?

Mine was ugly

so ugly.

Ugly.

Ugly.

Ugly.

She keeps mouthing the word 'Ugly', if it feels right she begins to sob

I should go. Come with?

SONNY. Ssssstay.

SONNY'S MUM. Don't Come In.

ROSHI. Who cares about your show!

SONNY. I-I care.

ROSHI. Cmonnn.

SONNY. I-I care!

ROSHI. Yous think you're gonna do this show and become an
artist?
That don't happen to people like us Sonny.

ROSHI *walks away.*
SONNY *clings onto her.*

SONNY. I'M GONNA HOLD MY BREATH UNTIL YOUS
STAY AND THEN WHEN I DIE IT'S GONNA BE YOUR
FAULT!!

ROSHI....

ROSHI *is now by the exit.*
SONNY *desperately begs.* ROSHI *exits.*

SONNY'S MUM. Don't Come In.

SONNY. Mum open the door!

SONNY'S MUM. Don't Come In.

SONNY. Why didn't I say more?

I should have said more.

SONNY'S MUM. I thought all the words in the universe
couldn't save me.

I was wrong.

I remember once
I heard you leave
You didn't have a coat on
And it is freezing outside.
And you didn't have a coat on.

I was on the edge of the bed
All I wanted was to be able to tell my son to put a coat on.
Because it was freezing outside and he doesn't have a coat
on.

Just let me do this.
Please let me do this one thing
Let me tell my son to put his coat on.

And then yous started to stammer and I was so scared
Did I do this?
Is this my fault? Have I broken him?

Will he be like me?
No
Don't let him be like me
Let him be good and pain-free
Let him look at the sky and not the ground.

There were no words for this.
Bury it down.
Bury bury bury it down.

SONNY. I'm in a school play Mum.

SONNY'S MUM. !!!

SONNY. I thought I lost somethin…

when yous
when yous
when yous

Died

SONNY'S MUM. If you lost something have you tried looking
for it?

SONNY. Yea.

SONNY'S MUM. And did you find it?

SONNY. I hadn't lost it.

SONNY'S MUM. You're gonna be late.

SONNY *looks to his mark scared.*

SONNY. I wish we could go home, build a fort and then say all the things we actually wanted.

SONNY'S MUM. I tried to stay.

I wanted to see you soar.

I wanted to see you soar so fucking bad baby.

SONNY. I miss you.

SONNY'S MUM. Remember the good days?

ROSHI *returns.*

ROSHI. Yous look ugly when yous cry.

SONNY. N-N-N-N-NOT CRYIN!

ROSHI. Yous still look ugly.

SONNY *looks to his mark scared.*

Yous never saw me.
I was never here.
Let's go.
Five.

ROSHI *takes* SONNY*'s hand.*
They take a small step to his mark.

Four.

Still holding his hand tightly she takes another small step with him.

Three.

I'll look after yous.
Like my dad said about my hamster, Colin,
'Yous didn't look after her so she died.'
But I'll look after yous, keep yous safe.

They pass WILLIAM SHAKESPEARE *who gets* SONNY *to sign his playtext.*
Maybe takes a selfie.

Two.

They pass CAPTAIN CHATTER.

SONNY. Yous can watch in the corner but be quiet.

ROSHI. One.

SONNY *passes his* MUM *so he can stand on his mark.*

SONNY'S MUM. There was a moment when I knew he would
be okay
It was just after his fifth birthday.
He's on the swing
and he doesn't need me to push him any more.
He's going higher and higher and higher and saying 'I'm
going to fly to the moon Mum!'
And I'm thinking yea, yous fly to the moon wonder boy
You fly to the moon

SONNY *breathes out and is about to speak.*

The stars above him

ever so reachable.

www.nickhernbooks.co.uk

facebook.com/nickhernbooks

twitter.com/nickhernbooks